READING
ETHNOGRAPHY

DAVID JACOBSON

STATE UNIVERSITY OF NEW YORK PRESS

Published by
State University of New York Press, Albany

© 1991 State University of New York

Printed in the United States of America

For information, address State University of New York
Press, State University Plaza, Albany, N.Y., 12246

Production by E. Moore
Marketing by Fran Keneston

Library of Congress Cataloging-in-Publication Data

Jacobson, David, 1940–
    Reading ethnography / David Jacobson.
        p. cm.
    Includes bibliographical references.
    ISBN 0-7914-0546-X (alk. paper). —ISBN 0-7914-0547-8 (pbk.:
alk. paper)
        1. Ethnology—Authorship.   2. Ethnology—Methodology.   I. Title.
GN307.7.J33 1991
305.8—dc20   90-35230
                                                                    CIP

10 9 8 7 6 5 4 3 2 1

READING
ETHNOGRAPHY

A man who makes an assertion puts forward a claim—a claim on our attention and on our belief . . . . Whatever the nature of the particular assertion may be . . . in each case we can challenge the assertion, and demand to have our attention drawn to the grounds (backing, data, facts, evidence, considerations, features) on which the merits of the assertion are to depend.

Stephen Edelston Toulmin,
The Uses of Argument, 1958:11

CONTENTS

ACKNOWLEDGMENTS

I thank Fredrik Barth and the Athlone Press for permission to reprint copyrighted material from *Political Leadership among Swat Pathans* and F. G. Bailey and the University of Manchester Press for permission to reprint copyrighted material from *Tribe, Caste, and Nation*. I also thank Grace Harris, Al Harris, and Bob Merrill, who first taught me to read ethnography. I have discussed the ideas that inform this book with friends and colleagues, and I am grateful to George Appell, Pat Harvey, Maurice Hershenson, Bob Hunt, David Kaplan, Bob Manners, David Murray, and Charles Ziegler for their advice and encouragement. George Appell, Al Harris, and Bob Manners were especially helpful in commenting on a draft of the manuscript. I also want to give credit to my family: Emily and Matthew have patiently listened to me talk about this book for a long time and have been sympathetic all the while; Ric, Sarah, and Abby, who have heard about it for a shorter period, also deserve thanks for their kind interest. Finally, I offer my deepest appreciation to my wife Lois whose unlimited and unflagging support has made it possible for me to complete this project.

Chapter 1

INTRODUCTION

This book is about reading ethnography. Clifford Geertz has written that "if you want to understand what a science is, you should look in the first instance not at its theories or its findings, and certainly not at what its apologists say about it; you should <u>look at what the practitioners of it do</u>," adding that in social anthropology "what the practitioners do is ethnography" (1973b:5). The Oxford English Dictionary states that "<u>ethnography</u>" is "the scientific description of nations," although <u>anthropologists generally define it as the description of behavior in a particular culture, typically resulting from fieldwork</u> (cf. Marcus and Cushman 1982, Boissevain 1985, Van Maanen 1988). Ethnographic accounts <u>usually take the form of an essay,</u> ordinarily published as an article in a professional journal or as a longer monograph, the scholarly report of the culture (or some aspect of the culture) of a specific people (cf. Geertz 1973b:25, Edgerton and Langness 1974:64, Thornton 1983). An ethnographic monograph is often simply referred to as an ethnography.

Given these definitions, readers may understandably approach an ethnography as if it were a simple account of a people, society, or culture. They may assume that an ethnographic monograph portrays directly, in an unfiltered fashion, the subject with which it is concerned. They may read an ethnography as if it were a documentary or a journalistic story, an example of straight reportage or the pretension that Geertz characterizes as "looking at the world directly, as through a one-way screen, seeing others as they really are when only God is looking" (Geertz 1988:141). When they read this way, however, they miss much of the meaning of the monograph and the significance of the ethnography it contains.

In fact, every ethnography involves interpretation and includes a selection of data, made more or less explicitly within a theoretical framework. Thus, the picture of the people, society, or culture that the ethnography presents must be understood from the perspective of (1) the question or problem that it addresses, (2) the answer, explanation, or interpretation it provides, (3) the data it includes as evidence for the problem, for the interpretation, or for both, and (4) the organization of these elements (problem, interpretation, and evidence) into an argument. To understand even the seemingly most straightforward ethnography, it is necessary to analyze and evaluate the argument(s) it contains. It is the goal of this book to help readers understand how to do that.

Recently there have been other efforts to deal with these issues. Marcus (1980) and his associates (Marcus and Cushman 1982 and Clifford and Marcus 1986), Clifford (1983, 1988), Geertz (1988), and Van Maanen (1988), among others, approach them from the point of view of assessing the rhetorical strategies and narrative conventions of writing ethnographic texts, while Holy and Stuchlik (1983) address them in the context of examining the methodology of anthropological inquiry, although each is concerned with a wider range of epistemological problems than I will take up. Their discussions significantly aid in understanding how to read ethnography, and I will refer to them frequently, especially with regard to matters of levels of analysis and textual organization, the two central topics of this book.

These contributions, however, raise points which call for clarification and further development. For example, Marcus and Cushman (1982:25–27) argue that a concern with the ways in which ethnographies are constructed and with "experimental" reactions to the conventions of presenting ethnography is a relatively recent interest among anthropologists, beginning in the early 1970s. The major problem with this formulation is that many ethnographies published between the 1920s and the 1960s gave explicit attention to the manner of composing ethnographic texts and attempted to experiment with ethnographic argumentation and textual organization (cf. Strathern 1987). These monographs include, among others, the classics produced by Malinowski (1922, 1926, 1935), Bateson (1936), Firth (1936), Evans-Pritchard (1937, 1940a, 1951a, 1956), Fortes (1945, 1949), Leach (1954, 1961), Barth (1959), and the anthropologists of the Manchester school (for example, Gluckman 1940, Mitchell 1956, Turner 1957, Bailey 1960, Cohen 1969).

Indeed, Firth, in reviewing the history of modern social anthropology, makes the point that the pioneers of social anthropology, as well as their students, were consciously and systematically innovative in writing up their fieldwork materials. He states that in the 1920s and 1930s the handling of fieldwork observations may not have been "highly abstract,"

> but in choice of topic, framework of presentation, and organization of data there was a tacit awareness of theoretical issues of a dynamic kind in social process. The treatment was novel if only because it rejected the then current orthodoxy that fact and theory should be clearly separated and the "facts" should be left to speak for themselves. . . . [The] "classics" in social anthropology . . . were experimental: in trying to provide more systematic and more relevant ethnography; in pointing to a range of theoretical problems calling for further exploration; and in testing, less successfully, the market for serious unglamorized information on basic social issues in communities with ways of life alien to the Western world (1975:4–5).

It may be that every generation of researchers thinks that it is not only building on the works of its predecessors but advancing beyond them, sometimes dramatically, and often by challenging the discipline's basic assumptions and established usages. However, portraying ethnographies, except for those produced by contemporary anthropologists, as uninventive theoretically, and as constrained by rigid conventions, is quite misleading. To fully appreciate current ethnographic accounts, it is useful to place them in context by comparing them with the ways in which the "classics" were written. To understand the construction of both classics and contemporary ethnographies, it is necessary to read them carefully and critically.

INTERPRETATION AND ANALYSIS

Understanding an ethnography begins with the recognition that it involves interpretation. Ethnographies do not merely depict the object of anthropological research, whether a people, a culture, or a society. Rather an ethnographic account constitutes the researcher's interpretation of what he or she has observed and/or heard. Fortes, in introducing what has become a classic ethnography, wrote,

> Writing an anthropological monograph is itself an instrument of research, and perhaps the most significant instrument of research in the anthropologist's armoury. It involves breaking up the vivid, kaleidoscopic reality of human action, thought, and emotion which lives in

the anthropologist's note-books and memory, and creating out of the pieces a coherent representation of a society . . . (1945:vii; cf. Fortes 1970b:129; Edgerton and Langness 1974:58).

Marcus and Cushman, more recently, have made essentially the same point. They state that:

> Ethnographic description is by no means the straightforward, unproblematic task it is thought to be in the social sciences, but a complex effect, achieved through writing and dependent upon the strategic choice and construction of available detail. The presentation of interpretation and analysis is inseparably bound up with the systematic and vivid representation of a world that seems total and real to the reader (1982:29).

An ethnography presents the anthropologist's interpretation (of some aspect) of the "reality of human action" and not merely a description of it.

The difference between description and interpretation is illuminated by considering ways in which anthropologists have distinguished between them. One well-known distinction is Geertz's differentiation (1973b) between "thin" and "thick" description. Thin description depicts behavior in the sense of physical motions, as seen, for example, by the eye of a camera; in contrast, thick description reveals its significance. Geertz uses the example of "twitches" and "winks" to illustrate this point (for other examples, cf. Schneider 1976:198, Holy and Stuchlik 1983:17). Both entail the same physical movement—the contraction of the muscles of the eyelid. A wink, however, conveys meaning: it may be a "conspiratorial" signal or some other message possible within the framework of a "socially established code."

According to Geertz, the object of ethnography as thick description is to understand the "frames of interpretation" within which behavior is classified and meaning is attributed to it. He argues (1973b:10) that this involves apprehending and depicting the "complex conceptual structures" in terms of which people behave and in terms of which that behavior is intelligible to them. Ethnography, then, is a matter of interpreting the meaning of behavior with reference to the cultural categories within which it is "produced, perceived, and interpreted." Winking exists, for example, "when there is a public code in which so doing counts as a conspiratorial signal" (Geertz 1973b:6), and, as he adds, "You can't wink . . . without knowing what counts as winking . . . " (1973b:12).

Although Geertz's formulation of the difference between description and interpretation is shared by many anthropologists, there is another view of the matter. Fortes (1970b [1953]), for example, provides a related but different conceptualization of description and interpretation. For Geertz, anthropological interpretation aims at discovering the cultural categories of a people and the "informal logic" (1973b:17; cf. Ortner 1984:130) of their social life that is embodied in those concepts. Fortes shares that goal, but, in addition, argues for a level of understanding that can go beyond that of the people whose behavior is in question (cf. Bailey 1969:9). Fortes's position extends the possibilities of anthropological interpretation to include an understanding of behavior that might differ from that of the people involved and would permit comparison of behavior in different societies and cultures.

To advance his argument, Fortes draws a distinction between "description" and "analysis." In a description, observations are grouped together as they actually happen. That is, they are included within an account in the order of their occurrence or because they occurred in the same place. Marriage, in an example used by Fortes, may be described as a sequence of customary activities succeeding one another in a set pattern, beginning with dating behavior, followed by courtship, betrothal, wedding ceremonies, and perhaps divorce as the event by which the relationship is terminated. The progression of these activities may be compressed, the periods between them condensed, but their relation to one another over time is preserved. The details of each activity may be presented more or less elaborately, but whatever attention is given to such particulars, the focus is on their sequence.

The procedure in analysis, in contrast to description, is to "break up the empirical sequence and concomitance of custom and social relations and group [them] . . . in categories of general import" (1970b:132). These categories are theoretically based. The task is to examine behavior in terms of these analytical categories and the relationships among them. "Rights" and "duties" are examples of such theoretical categories. They are aspects of a role, the culturally defined and socially sanctioned expectations or claims regarding the behavior of those who interact with one another. What people do, or fail to do, is interpreted in terms of such rights and duties.

The difference between description and analysis can be illustrated in the case of "bridewealth," an event that occurs in marriages in many societies. Bridewealth entails the transfer of wealth from the group of the groom to that of the bride. From one perspective, bridewealth may be seen as compensation paid to one group for the loss of a woman, a view that seems to accord with the observation that such wealth is typically used by the group that receives it to acquire another woman, as a bride for one of its members. This sort of account is essentially descriptive. An alternative account follows from an analysis of bridewealth. It would assert that bridewealth is paid to acquire certain rights with respect to a woman's activities. Bridewealth, from this perspective, is not for the exchange of individuals, but for the transfer of rights or claims upon the services of individuals.

This way of viewing bridewealth helps to make sense of a wide range of observations. It brings out clearly the theoretical meaning of descriptive data. For example, Fortes suggests that if a woman is thought of in terms of the roles of wife and mother, then it is possible to identify several types of behavior expected of her. These include domestic and sexual activities associated with being a wife and childbearing associated with being a mother. In a patrilineal society, in which children are assigned membership in the group of their father, the groom acquires, with regard to his spouse, rights in her as both wife and mother, and, accordingly, the amount of bridewealth is typically large. By contrast, in a matrilineal society, in which children are assigned to the group of their mother, the husband has a claim on the woman only in her role as a wife, while rights to her in the role of a mother are retained by the group into which she was born. Accordingly, bridewealth payments in matrilineal societies are typically smaller than they are in patrilineal societies. Thus, an analytical account of bridewealth relates variations in its amount to the type of society in which it occurs (that is, patrilineal or matrilineal), rather than seeing it simply as one event in a sequence of events that constitute marriage.

Furthermore, interpreting bridewealth as the exchange of resources for claims on a woman with respect to different roles permits the analyst to make connections between observations that are not obviously or closely associated with one another temporally. For example, it not only implies relationships between types of society and amounts of bridewealth but also between those social facts and rates of divorce. Thus, in a patrilineal society it would be expected analytically that not only would bridewealth payments be relatively high but that divorce would be relatively low. This pattern would be expected because the husband's group would not want to relinquish claims over a woman who, in her role as mother, is or will become the producer of its new members. On the other hand, in a matrilineal society, a woman of the group (a mother, a sister, or a daughter) is the source of new members; an in-marrying wife does not contribute new members for her husband's group. Correspondingly, in a matrilineal society, bridewealth may be expected to be low and divorce rates relatively high.

From an analytical perspective, then, the meaning of bridewealth is to be understood in the context of the rights and duties associated with different roles and the ways in which they can be distributed and combined. Rights and duties are abstractions formulated by the analyst, although, as Fortes noted, they "must have meaning in terms of the descriptive reality of social life" (1970b:132; cf. Schneider 1976:198–99). These categories or concepts are not necessarily those of the actors, and an analytical interpretation of behavior may not be the same as that held by the actors nor as an interpretation based solely upon an explication of the actors' categories (cf.

Geertz 1976:223–24, on "experience-near" and "experience-distant" concepts and the relationships between them). This is not to say that analysis does not consider cultural categories; rather, it typically takes them as a starting point for analysis, since what counts, for example, as a "marriage" or as "bridewealth" is to be understood in terms of the ways in which people classify such events and behaviors (cf. D'Andrade 1984:90–91).

ETHNOGRAPHIES AS ARGUMENTS

As Fortes noted, anthropologists not only "break up" or analyze the reality of human action, they also attempt to provide a coherent representation of it. This representation is an interpretive conclusion, and the descriptive facts (for example, marriage customs and bridewealth payments) collected in the course of fieldwork and included within an ethnography constitute evidence in support of it. That is, the anthropologist's interpretation determines his or her selection of fieldwork observations for inclusion in an ethnographic account. The selection and presentation of facts in an ethnography is a result of analysis and interpretation and not simply a record of observations made during the anthropologist's fieldwork.

Edgerton and Langness (1974) address this issue in referring to the process by which the observations that constitute an ethnographic description are selected. These observations are selected "twice." First, observations are "shaped" in terms of what anthropologists "see" in the field, which is filtered through the "personal equation" of the ethnographer. This includes, among other things, the anthropologist's personality, training, and theoretical interests. The interests of the people among whom the anthropologist is doing research also shape what the anthropologist may observe, since they can and do restrict the researcher's access to people and events. For example, male researchers may not be permitted to talk with women informants or to observe activities that are defined by informants as exclusively for women, and, of course, female anthropologists may be similarly constrained from doing fieldwork among male informants (cf. Whitehead and Conaway 1986).

Observations are also selected in terms of the anthropologist's representation of a people, culture, or society. This, in the language of Edgerton and Langness, is the second way in which the observations in an ethnographic monograph are filtered. They are chosen in relation to the analytical interests of the ethnographer and to the interpretation he or she is presenting. In other words, an ethnography constitutes an argument.

An argument, following Toulmin, involves "claims," "data," and "warrants" (1958:97–98; cf. Toulmin 1979). Thus, an argument consists of a claim or conclusion (C) and the data or grounds (D) that provide a foundation for the claim. It also includes warrants, which are steps that link con-clusions and data and which take the form of "If D, then C." Toulmin sug-gests that these warrants can be expressed more fully and more explicitly as "Data such as D entitle one to draw conclusions, or make claims, such as C, or alternatively, Given data D, one may take it that C." That is, warrants address the question of whether the data or grounds provide genuine support for a particular claim and not just a lot of irrelevant information. Ethno-graphic arguments consist of claims (conclusions, assertions, propositions, explanations, interpretations) about people's behavior (or about a culture or a society) and data (grounds, facts) that constitute evidence for or against them. An ethnography has a point of view, and it includes and excludes data in terms of their relevance to that point of view.

Thus, reading ethnography means, in part, identifying an ethnogra-phy's claims and evaluating them with reference to the data presented in support of them. In contrast to the perspective embodied in recent accounts of reflexive ethnography (which I address in the concluding chapter), this book takes a claims and evidence approach to assessing ethnography, focus-ing on what Roth (1989:560) characterizes as "questions of method," that is, the conditions under which "evidence cited supports a claim."

As arguments, ethnographies are problem oriented. Marcus and Cush-man argue for this view of ethnography, although they assert that it is more characteristic of current monographs than of earlier fieldwork reports. They write that in ethnography, "the contemporary fashion, dominated by more problem-focused research, is the single volume tied to a period of fieldwork and combining several complex descriptive and interpretive tasks" (1982:27). Again, this seems to underestimate the purposes and achieve-ments of the monographs of an earlier era. Evans-Pritchard's discussion of the nature of anthropological monographs, published some three decades before that of Marcus and Cushman, places this issue in historical perspec-tive. He wrote:

> The essential point to remember is that the anthropologist is working with a body of theoretical knowledge and that he makes his observa-tions to solve problems which derive from it. . . . Modern fieldwork monographs are generally intended to give more than merely a description of the social life of a people. . . . They aim at an analytical and integrative description which will bring out those features of the social life which are significant for an understanding of its structure and for general theory. . . . It means that the facts, that is, the observa-tions recorded in the anthropologist's notebooks, are not set forth in his publications as a description of what a primitive people do and say, but to show that what they do and say, apart from its intrinsic interest,

illuminates some problem of one or other aspect of culture or institutional life. In other words, in deciding what he is to put into his book and what to leave out of it, he is guided by the relevance of the material for a particular theme designed to bring out significant features of some system of social activities (1951b:87–88; cf. Fortes 1970b:129).

LEVELS OF ANALYSIS

Analyzing the kinds of claims and the kinds of data included within an ethnography and examining the extent to which they warrant each other is one of the central tasks in reading an ethnography. Anthropologists make different kinds of claims about the people they observe. These differences derive from the ways in which anthropologists conceptualize the object of their fieldwork; they study different "domains of social reality" and work at different "levels of analysis" (Holy and Stuchlik 1983; cf. Fortes 1970b:136; Schneider 1976:202). That is not to say that there are different social realities, but rather that anthropologists write ethnographies that reflect different abstractions from observable behavior. The ways in which anthropologists approach social reality shape the kinds of claims they make about it and the kinds of data they include in their ethnographies.

Several observers have noted that there are two major ways in which anthropologists, and other social scientists as well, conceptualize social reality. Firth, for example, differentiates these levels of analysis as focusing on "modes of thought" or "modes of action" (1975:8). Holy and Stuchlik (1983:20–21), to take another example, suggest that some anthropologists focus on "culture," others on "social structure." These differences are also described by other sets of contrasting terms, including methodological collectivism and methodological individualism, concepts and actions, theory and practice, structure and process (cf., Fortes 1970c [1949]; Firth 1954, 1955, 1975; Leach 1954, 1961; Goodenough 1970; Barnes 1971; O'Neill 1973; Keesing 1974; Geertz 1976; Schneider 1968, 1976; D'Andrade 1984).

The multiplicity of terms anthropologists employ in referring to these levels of analysis can confuse the reader of an ethnography in at least two ways. One difficulty derives from the use of different concepts to refer to the same level of analysis. Confusion may also follow from the fact that the same term may be used to describe different levels of analysis. For example, some anthropologists use the term structure to refer to an ideational system and others use it to refer to a system of actions (e.g., Evans-Pritchard 1940a for the former; Fortes 1970c and Firth 1954, 1955 [reprinted in 1964a as chapters 2 and 3] for the latter; cf. Leach 1961:5 on the different referents of the term social structure). Reading ethnography critically requires paying careful attention to such concepts and to their particular referents in different ethnographic accounts.

Researchers who take modes of thought (or culture or theory, and so forth) as the focus of analysis and description present a system of ideas or notions that is said to guide the actions of individuals and/or provide them with standards in terms of which they interpret or make sense out of their own actions and those of others. Those who make modes of action (or process or practice, and so forth) the focus of study describe the actual behavior of individuals, interpreting such behavior with reference to the ideas of those engaged in them but also with reference to other factors as well, including, for example, environmental constraints on behavior.

Modes of thought ethnographies may focus on two different aspects. One refers to the way in which people classify or conceptualize their world. Anthropologists use different terms to refer to these classifications, including "cultural categories" or "conceptions" (Geertz 1973b:7, 15), "representations" (Holy and Stuchlik 1983:50–54; Schneider 1976:206), and "cultural units" (Schneider 1976:199), which, in Schneider's language, reflect a "body of definitions, premises, statements, postulates, presumptions, propositions, and perceptions about the nature of the universe and man's place in it" (Schneider 1976:203; cf. 206). The other aspect refers to the ways in which people should act, ought to act, or are expected to act. Anthropologists describe these expectations as "normative rules" or "norms" (Schneider 1976:199; Holy and Stuchlik 1983:52–53). D'Andrade states the difference between cultural categories and norms "as a contrast between ideas that create realities and ideas that order or constrain action" (1984:93; cf. Geertz's distinction between "models of" and "models for" in "Religion as A Cultural System," 1973c). Other anthropologists, as well as different social scientists and philosophers, use still other terms to denote these different aspects of modes of thought (cf. Holy and Stuchlik 1983:50; D'Andrade 1984:90–96).

These approaches to social reality are not mutually exclusive. Rather they are complementary, and many, if not most, anthropologists incorporate both analytical levels in their ethnographies, taking as problematic the relationships between them. Yet, it is useful for identifying the type(s) of argument(s) an ethnography contains to consider these different approaches to social reality as the endpoints of a continuum and to examine the extent to which the claims of ethnographies vary, or are differentially emphasized, depending on whether they are more concerned with concepts about or rules for behavior, on the one hand, or with actual behavior on the other. It is useful to identify the level of analysis or the sort of social reality an ethnography depicts, because different levels of analysis or conceptualizations of social reality imply the use of different kinds of data, and different kinds of data warrant different kinds of claims and/or conclusions.

CLAIMS AND DATA

The claims made in an ethnography may be evaluated in at least three ways. Two of these involve comparison with materials outside or beyond the limits of the specific ethnographic account in question. An ethnographic account can be compared with accounts of other societies that are similar, geographically, culturally, or organizationally, thereby providing a framework for evaluating its interpretation. That is, a reader can draw on knowledge of other related societies and estimate the probability of the accuracy of the ethnography in question, always keeping in mind the provision that societies initially thought to be similar may turn out, on the basis of further investigation, to be otherwise. The principle here is that if other systems are similar in some respects, then they may be similar in still others. If an ethnographic account does not make sense in this commonsensical way, then the reader should resort to still other checks on its validity.

Another approach is to compare a particular ethnographic account with reports about the same society (or culture, or whatever may be the unit of analysis and description) prepared by other researchers. Here the reader may consult the entire corpus of information available about a society, including accounts generated by anthropologists as well as others (for example, travelers, missionaries, administrators, and so forth). The strategy here is to place one ethnographic account within a context of others' observations on the same society.

The third way of assessing an ethnographic account is to evaluate the interpretation internally. From this perspective, the reader tests the fit between the ethnographer's interpretations and the evidence presented within the ethnographic account.

The presentation of appropriate and relevant evidence is critical to the construction and evaluation of ethnographic arguments. As Firth put it:

Social anthropology is not just an exercise in speculative reasoning. It is about the actions and thoughts of people over a range of societies. So when any statement is made about such actions and thoughts, a very proper question is, what is the nature of the evidence? (1975:18; cf. Edgerton and Langness 1974:59).

What kinds of evidence do anthropologists present in their ethnographies? Holy and Stuchlik suggest that "there are two broad categories of data: the verbal statements of the members of the society and their observed behavior" (1983:12). Difficulties in interpretation arise when the differences between these types of evidence are disregarded or when the different types of data are taken to refer to the same kind of social reality.

Typically, anthropologists use verbal data to make claims about modes of thought and nonverbal data to make claims about modes of action. That is, interpretations of ideational systems are usually based upon observations of what people say and interpretations of systems of action are based upon observations of what people do. However, drawing this distinction between types of data is a heuristic device and matters are usually more complicated. For example, as Holy and Stuchlik point out, "actions are often accompanied by statements, without which they would be incomplete," and, furthermore, that there is a category of statements, performatives, "which, merely by being uttered, 'do' the intended thing..." (1983:56; cf. Searle 1969). This distinction, then, is not to suggest that talk is not a kind of behavior, but rather that anthropologists distinguish between what people say and what they do and use these different types of data to document their claims about different domains or levels of analysis.

MODES OF THOUGHT AND LINGUISTIC EVIDENCE

In interpreting a people's modes of thought, anthropologists have relied "largely if not exclusively on linguistic data" (Firth 1975:8; cf. Firth 1985:36–37, Holy and Stuchlik 1983:74). Verbal behavior includes what people say about the way the world is (cultural categories) and what they say about how people ought to act in it (norms).

People's words constitute the primary evidence for cultural categories or representations. In ethnographies these are sometimes referred to as native terms or indigenous concepts. Anthropologists have developed different research methodologies for eliciting and analyzing such data (Holy and Stuchlik 1983:60–68). In most ethnographies, however, native terms (conventionally presented in italicized print) are presented as evidence of a people's concepts and explained or translated by the ethnographer. For example, in the course of discussing what people in different societies think persons are, Geertz (1976) uses native terms as the basis of his arguments about the cross-cultural meanings of self. Thus, he claims that the "Javanese sense of what a person is" is evident in two sets of contrasting terms, *lair* and *batin* and *alus* and *kasar*, glossed as "inside" and "outside" and "refined" and "rough," that refer to "the felt realm of human experience . . . and the observed realm of human behavior" (1976:226). Similarly, Geertz argues that the Balinese sense of personhood is seen in their "terminological system" that constitutes "a set of readily observable symbolic forms: an elaborate repertoire of designations and titles" (1976:228). And for Moroccans, ideas about self can be seen in "a peculiar linguistic form called in Arabic the *nisba*," by means of which they "sort people out from one another and form an idea of what it is to be a person" (1976:231).

In short, the reader of an ethnography should be aware that the inclusion in it of native terms is most likely not accidental or arbitrary, but because they provide evidence for claims about cultural categories. It should be noted that the presentation of native terms as evidence for claims about the ways in which people conceptualize their world has a long history in ethnography. It is not, as Marcus and Cushman suggest (1982:36), only a feature of recent experimental monographs. Evans-Pritchard (1940a) and Leach (1954), for example, do not fall within the group of recent and experimental ethnographers mentioned by Marcus and Cushman, although they certainly engaged in the "contextual exegesis of native concepts."

Although anthropologists use verbal data as the primary evidence for assertions about modes of thought, they also employ other symbols for the same purpose. Just as cultural categories are expressed in words, they can also be concretized in various material objects. As D'Andrade notes, "flags, capitals and uniforms are treated as the embodiments of a nation-state, paper bills are treated as embodiments of wealth, signatures are considered to represent personal commitment" (1984:92). Of course, the meanings of such "physical tokens" do not reside in them and their significance is not self-evident. Anthropologists must interpret physical objects just as they interpret physical movements.

Interpreting or translating a cultural category or concept, or its embodiment in a physical token, is, however, a complex task. It involves understanding the ideational system of which it is a part. Beidelman draws attention to this point in his discussion of Evans-Pritchard's analysis of the Nuer concept of marriage. He writes:

> The term marriage, as used by Evans-Pritchard in reference to the Nuer, obviously does not stand for the customs, rights, and obligations which we associate with marriage in our society. But this is only the beginning of the problem. For to understand Nuer marriage we must also understand the more basic Nuer notions which support and rationalize Nuer norms surrounding the various aspects of marital relations, such as notions of fertility, paternity, maternity, masculinity, femininity, descent, and physiology. As Evans-Pritchard has shown, these, in turn, involve complex association with Nuer concepts of time, death, spirit, and morality. According to this point of view, then, a complete exegesis of an alien cosmology is required before one may even begin to fathom the norms and goals held by members of a society (1970:511; cf. Fortes 1970b:137; Geertz 1973b:9; Holy and Stuchlik 1983:59; D'Andrade 1984:93).

Understanding a concept within a context that is itself a system of concepts poses certain methodological problems that will be discussed in more detail in later chapters. For the moment, however, it is important to note that such concepts constitute data in support of claims about the ways in which people think.

Claims about norms also entail verbal data, but usually they involve people's statements about how they and others should or should not act. Such statements include naturally occurring prescriptions and proscriptions as well as responses to questions posed by others. Sometimes a normative rule is stated as though it were a description of what people do. For example, people may say that "drivers stop at red lights," which is an obligation or an expected pattern of behavior, but which is not necessarily or actually what they do.

Anthropologists are concerned with the relationship between norms and actions, although there are different perspectives on that relationship (cf. Holy and Stuchlik 1983:71–75, 81–98). Some anthropologists, following Durkheim, argue that norms cannot be simply inferred from actions, since actions may also be shaped by nonnormative factors. For example, Peristiany, in commenting on the work of Durkheim, points out that one level of social reality does not directly mirror the other. Thus, he notes, observations that most marriages are monogamous does not permit the inference that polygamy is not allowed or even that it is not the ideal, since monogamy may result from nonnormative factors; that is, it "may be due to reasons which are fortuitous in relation to the system of social beliefs" (Peristiany 1974:xv).

Others contend that norms can also be inferred from observations of what people do. Holy and Stuchlik, for example, hold this view. They write:

> While representations . . . are available to the researcher, by and large, only through people's verbal statements, . . . norms, rules, etc., can be inferred from both verbal statements and observed actions. . . . Assuming that all actions are guided by relevant knowledge, and are meaningful to others because the actor and the others share the same notions, it follows that by observing actions . . . and by accounting for them as meaningful, the anthropologist should be able to infer the notions guiding these actions (1983:68).

This assumption is not shared by all fieldworkers, and most anthropologists appear to base their claims about normative rules primarily on verbal data, and especially on what people say about how they and others should or ought to act.

MODES OF ACTION AND BEHAVIORAL EVIDENCE

To support claims about what people do, anthropologists resort to a different kind of evidence. They use censuses and statistics that summarize people's actions by frequency and distribution. For example, Fortes (1970c) describes variations in household composition as part of his analysis of the developmental cycle of domestic groups. They also use "case" material, which includes observations of particular individuals interacting in specific situations. These observations may be made by the fieldworker, by others (as reports of actions), or both.

Case material, in turn, includes various kinds of observations. A case may illustrate a particular norm; that is, it depicts individuals behaving in relation to cultural ideas about how people should act. Cases may also depict social processes. Thus, a case might show how individuals choose to behave when faced with alternative norms and/or when constrained by nonnormative factors such as ecological conditions. This use of case material depicts action at one point in time. Cases can also be used to document action over time, a procedure called "situational analysis" or "the extended case method" (cf. Gluckman 1961, Van Velsen 1967). When used in this way, the same individuals are described acting in different situations. By holding constant the individuals involved in interaction (and assuming that they have not undergone a significant change of personality or personal style of behaving within a particular role), the extended case method enables the researcher to analyze the influence of different social situations or contexts on behavior. It also permits analysis of the impact on present behavior and relationships of past events and interactions as perceived by those involved in them, as well as that of future events and relationships as anticipated by actors.

It should be emphasized that the description of actions, whether as outcomes or as cases, implies cultural analysis. Describing what a person does is not simply an account of that individual's physical movements, but rather an analysis of the meaning of those movements. And although the meaning(s) of a movement may be attributed to it by the actor, by the analyst, or by both, in practice anthropologists take the actor's classification of behavior as the starting point of ethnographic description. Otherwise, the task of ethnography would be either impossible or its results inconsequential. As Holy and Stuchlik state:

> no study of action is possible without paying attention to the notions, concepts, and ideas related to it. . . . To circumscribe the study of actions . . . [without reference to cultural analysis] would mean that the whole research would be reduced to trivial descriptions of physical movements. . . . If we do not want simply to observe and report physical movements of people in temporal and spatial sequences, but to study and explain their actions, we can do it only by relating them, implicitly or explicitly, to some notions about such movements, to knowledge, beliefs, ideas or ideals, etc. In practical terms, this means

that even when we talk about the study of actions we are necessarily talking about some relationship between actions and notions (1983:35–36).

Accounts of what people do build upon accounts of what they think.

OTHER KINDS OF EVIDENCE

Ethnographies often contain data about a people's environment and their ecology. These facts are included because they are relevant to an account of what people do. Just as social norms influence actions, natural constraints define alternative courses of behavior and limit or facilitate particular choices. Indeed, it is important to consider both environmental and cultural factors when interpreting what people do; otherwise, significance may be wrongly attributed to, or undue emphasis placed upon, one or the other of these factors as a cause of a particular pattern of behavior. This is not to suggest that the natural environment automatically determines behavior, but that people choose from among alternatives as these are shaped by it. Moreover, visual data, such as photographs and line-drawings, may be incorporated into ethnographies as evidence for claims about ecological and environmental factors as well as about the people themselves, their artifacts, technologies, and activities. Evans-Pritchard, for example, included in his study of a pastoral people (*The Nuer*, 1940a) a number of drawings (Figures 7 and 13) and photographs (the Frontispiece and Plates III, V, and XVII), as illustration of the "identification of man with cattle," suggesting that they "present a classic picture of savagery" and "convey to [the reader] better than I can do in words the crudity of kraal life" (1940a:40–41). It should be noted, however, that although photographs can depict persons or settlement patterns, they do not provide direct evidence of the ways in which people think about how they ought to behave toward one another. Thus, while a profusion of visual material in an ethnography could support propositions about environment, material culture, and activities, it does not follow that propositions about social relationships are thereby documented.

WARRANTS

The two levels of analysis, modes of thought and modes of action, are not necessarily in a one-to-one relationship with one another. Barnes has made the point that verbal evidence supports claims about what people "would like to do, think it would be right to do, or expect they will do"

(1971:31). Yet he also indicates that there is often a discrepancy between the ideal and the real, and that the "picture of social life built up from one point of view may differ radically from that built up from another" (1971:31). Thus, the reader of an ethnography has to sort out kinds of claims and kinds of evidence, making certain that the type of evidence provided is appropriate to the type of claim made: that is, that linguistic evidence is used in relation to propositions about modes of thought and that behavioral data are used to support claims about actions. The presentation of verbal data is irrelevant to a conclusion about what people do (except when the claim is about the frequency and distribution of speech events) and evidence about what people do does not necessarily reveal what people think is ideal or preferred behavior. Correspondingly, rejection of a claim about a mode of thought on the basis of the absence of behavioral data is as inappropriate as is acceptance of propositions about action on the basis of what people say about what they do or should do.

ARGUMENT AND TEXTUAL ORGANIZATION

Although a primary consideration in reading an ethnography is to comprehend its level of analysis and the relationship between its claims and data, it is also essential to examine its textual organization, that is, the ways in which its problems, interpretations, and data are put together. This approach to reading ethnography is based on analytical frameworks suggested both outside and within anthropology. For example, Adler has drawn attention to it in his classic, *How to Read a Book* (1940), and, within anthropology, Marcus and Cushman (1982), Clifford (1983), Strathern (1987), and Geertz (1988) have addressed these issues.

According to Adler, there are two central tasks in studying the textual organization of any book. One is to identify its "unity" or its "theme," which is what the book is about. He also conceptualizes this as specifying a book's "problems" or "questions," in the sense that a book is written to solve a problem and that it "ostensibly contains one or more answers to it" (Adler 1940:183). This may be more difficult to do than it sounds, since, as Adler points out (1940:183):

The writer may or may not tell you what the questions were as well as give you the answers which are the fruits of his work. Whether he does or does not, and especially if he does not, it is your task as a reader to formulate the problems as precisely as you can.

Moreover, as he also states (1940:166–167):

Sometimes an author obligingly tells you on the title page what the unity is. . . . Sometimes the author tells you the unity of his plan in his preface. . . . Do not be too proud to accept the author's help if he proffers it, but do not rely too completely on what he says in the preface. The best-laid plans of authors, like those of other mice and men, gang aft agley. Be somewhat guided by the prospectus the author gives you, but always remember that the obligation of finding the unity belongs to the reader, as much as having one belongs to the writer.

The other task is to identify a book's "parts" and their relationships to its theme and to one another. Adler expresses this task in a rule for readers: "*Set forth the major parts of the book, and show how these are organized into a whole, by being ordered to one another and to the unity of the whole*" (1940:163). He argues (1940:171) that it is difficult, if not impossible, for the reader to understand a book unless he or she grasps the relationships between a book's unity and its parts: "You cannot apprehend a whole without somehow seeing its parts. But it is also true that unless you grasp the organization of its parts, you cannot know the whole comprehensively."

Reading ethnography confirms Adler's analysis of the architecture of textual construction. Ethnographic arguments are arranged in different ways, but each reveals a pattern of relationships between a problem and its solution. For example, the functionalist goal of representing a culture as a system of related, if not integrated, parts led ethnographers to "the obvious solution to the problem of textual organization," which was, according to Marcus and Cushman (1982:31; cf. Kaberry 1957:76–80, Edgerton and Langness 1974:65–66),

to traverse, in sequential fashion, the units (cultural complexes or social institutions) into which cultures or societies were conceived, on theoretical grounds, to be divided. The result was the minimally orthodox table of contents (geography, kinship, economics, politics, and religion).

Although this seriatim formula characterized many ethnographic texts for many years, and continues to do so today (primarily in a popular series of abbreviated ethnographies), other formats have been developed, including that of posing a problematic feature of the society or culture in question in the beginning of an ethnography and unfolding a solution to it in its subsequent chapters (cf. Marcus and Cushman 1982:31).

While it may be true that these particular efforts depart from the traditional organization of ethnographic monographs, it is not the case that such innovations are limited to recent works (cf. Strathern 1987). Several older ethnographic accounts (e.g., Malinowski 1922, Bateson 1936, Gluckman 1940, Wilson 1951, Evans-Pritchard 1962), employed a strategy of interpreting an apparently unintelligible behavior (a practice, a ritual, an event, a social pattern, or a concept) by placing it in a wider context, although what constituted that context varied. Still others (for example, Evans-Pritchard 1940a) reversed that strategy by first describing a social context and then placing some behavior in it (in this instance, the institution of the feud), thereby explaining its function or meaning. Marcus and Cushman acknowledge these pioneering and experimental ventures in ethnographic textual organization (1982:40), although they downplay both the number of these studies and the impact they had on the practice of writing ethnography.

In sum, the problem and the solution of a book shape the organization of its parts, and the order of its parts reflects its problem and solution. Analyzing the textual organization of an ethnography raises several questions: Why is a particular topic or chapter included within an ethnographic monograph? What is its role in the overall argument? Why is it placed in its particular position (for example, in the beginning, middle, or end of an ethnographic account)? and What are the relationships among the constituent topics or chapters of an ethnography? In short, it is essential to read an ethnography as an argument, and to view the arrangement of its chapters as steps in support of its interpretive conclusions.

A brief examination of Liebow's Tally's Corner (1967) provides an illustration of ethnographic textual organization.

I use it as an example not only because it is a well-known and well-written ethnography, but also because the people it describes are low-income black men living, at the time of Liebow's fieldwork, in Washington, D.C. Their language and their customs are not foreign to us, and analyzing the architecture of the monograph is made easier since we do not have to sort out unfamiliar cultural categories and social norms.

Tally's Corner is about a "shifting collection" of men who hang out on a ghetto street corner. Tally is one of those men; in the course of the fieldwork, he and Liebow become friends. It is also about the social and economic conditions that influence men's lives. Indeed, it is Liebow's argument that the behavior of the men whom he came to know is explained by a combination of conditions of poverty (a lack of education, job skills, and material resources) and a system of values common to society in general, rather than by "mute compliance" with a patholological "subculture" which sets them apart, ineradicably, from their fellow citizens. To support this interpretation, he develops his argument along two lines. One is to describe the circumstances of a life of chronic material deficits. The other is to describe the values of these men, including the desire for respectability, as essentially the same as those of middle-class Americans.

Liebow's initial step is to establish the facts of their economic deprivation. Early in the book, in a chapter entitled "Men and Jobs," Liebow presents the data for his claims about their work experiences and economic resources. There he also begins his account of their values by analyzing the meanings that they attach to their jobs. In both cases, Liebow demonstrates that their standards of evaluation are similar to those of the middle class; only their job experiences and the occupational opportunities they envision are different. The prime position that Liebow gives to poverty as an explanatory factor suggests that he thinks that it is (and should be) the first target of intervention for public policies intended to change the lives of lower-class Americans, a theme to which he returns more explicitly in the conclusion of the study.

Thus, in the beginning of the ethnography Liebow develops his view that behavior is to be understood in terms of an interaction between responsibilities (as these are evident in the work role), the resources necessary to fulfill them, and the respectability that accrues from doing so. When resources are inadequate for discharging responsibilities, the result is, typically, a loss of self-respect and the respect of others. The combination inevitably influences the individual's behavior in a number of ways.

Having shown this to be the case in man-job relationships, Liebow continues the examination of this proposition in succeeding chapters on other relationships, namely those in which men play roles as fathers, husbands, lovers, and friends. As Liebow reiterates in his conclusion, "The way in which the man makes a living and the kind of living he makes have important consequences for how the man sees himself and is seen by others; and these, in turn, importantly shape his relationships with family members, lovers, friends and neighbors" (1967:210). The particular sequence of these chapters reinforces Liebow's interpretation as he progresses from ascribed roles to achieved roles, from those in which the obligations (or responsibilities) to provide resources is strongest—legally, publically, and socially—to those in which it is weakest.

For these men, the relationships in which they are most expected to be providers are those in which they are least likely to succeed. Their perception of such a dismal prospect pushes them into various self-defeating courses of action. For example, Liebow writes: "In theory, marriage is a "big thing"; it is the way to manhood with all its attendant responsibilities, duties, and obligations, which, when discharged, bring one status and respectability" (1967:115). Yet, Liebow argues, it is a goal that commonly escapes these men, since chronic poverty undermines their attempts to provide for a wife and children.

Liebow's analysis of the broken marriages of these men reveals most clearly his argument that it is an inadequacy of resources in conjunction with mainstream values, rather than a distinctive set of cultural rules or social norms, that accounts for behavior among these street corner men. He writes:

> the succession of mates which characterizes marriage . . . does not constitute a distinctive cultural pattern "with an integrity of its own." It is rather the cultural model of the larger society as seen through the prism of repeated failure. Indeed, it might be more profitable . . . to look on marriage as a succession of failures rather than as a succession of mates (1967:221).

In short, the organization of Liebow's ethnography contributes to the conclusion that for the men he came to know it is the interplay of economic constraints and cultural values that shape their behavior and make it intelligible.

CHANGING MODES OF ANALYSIS IN ETHNOGRAPHIC STUDIES

The history of ethnographic writing reveals a pattern in which there is an alternation of emphasis from one level of analysis (or domain of social reality) to the other (cf. Kaberry 1957, Gluckman 1961, Van Velsen 1967, Cohen 1974, Firth 1975 and 1985, Basso and Selby 1976, Crick 1976, Vincent 1978, and Ortner 1984). Ethnographies of the last seventy years or so can be placed in five overlapping, but analytically separable, phases or periods.

"Functional" ethnographies, written by Malinowski and his students from the early 1920s through the middle 1930s, emphasized the actual behavior of individuals. In them, as Kaberry remarks, we learn about individuals as "actors in a changing scene, as individuals who co-operate, quarrel, cheat, compromise, give generously, contradict one another . . . , diverge from the rules, pay the penalty or sometimes avoid it" (1957:71).

"Structural" studies, deriving from the work of Radcliffe-Brown, had their heyday in the period from the early 1930s through the early 1950s. They focused on modes of thought and especially on social roles and norms. Van Velsen (1967:131) points out that structural ethnographies "are primarily concerned with relations between social positions or statuses rather than with the 'actual relations' . . . or 'behavior'" of specific individuals. "This type of analysis," he remarks, "does not allow for the fact that individuals are often faced by a choice between alternative norms" (1967:131). Comparing functional and structural ethnographies, Kaberry (1957:88) comments that "many structural studies carry only a light ballast of ethnographic content," adding that the "people, in the sense of a group of personalities, are conspicuous by their absence."

"Processual" ethnography was a reaction to the emphasis on normative rules in structural studies. It included several variants, sometimes referred to as "conflict" or "transactional" anthropology, and dealt with problems of "social organization," as Firth (1951, 1954) described it. This style of ethnography focused on individuals' actions and especially on the ways in which they choose between alternative courses of action. It extended and refined the use of case materials, emphasizing the analysis of social process, "the way in which individuals actually handle their structural relationships and exploit the element of choice between alternative norms according to the requirements of any particular situation" (Van Velsen 1967:148). Processual ethnography became strong in the middle 1950s and continued to be a significant style through the middle 1960s.

"Cultural" analyses took the place of transactional ethnographies and focused on questions of "meaning." This style of ethnography flourished between the early 1960s and the late 1970s. As noted in discussing Geertz's view of interpretation (1973b:12), the aim of this sort of ethnography is to analyze the "socially established structures of meaning" that render behavior intelligible. In this phase, too, there were several variants, including those differentiated by the terms "symbolic," "cognitive," and, again, "structural" studies. Although the "structural" studies of the 1960s and 1970s employ the same term as those of an earlier phase, there are significant theoretical differences between them. Fortes (1978:9, note 4) refers to "anglo- or socio-structuralism, i.e., the structural-functionalism, derived from Radcliffe-Brown and those of us who worked with him, and the gallo- or linguo-structuralism of Levi-Strauss and his followers."

Firth, writing in the middle 1970s, thought that a new emphasis was emerging, a phase of "neo-empiricism," which would give "renewed attention" to the study of people's actions. He coined the term "logistical anthropology" to describe this phase (1975:19–21). More recently, Firth (1985:43) has further outlined the characteristics of an action-oriented anthropology which he calls "rheological anthropology."

Ortner's examination (1984) of theoretical developments in anthropology since the 1960s, although tracing more lines of analysis than Firth did, generally supports his earlier classification. She sees anthropological studies moving from the symbolic and gallo-structural studies of the early 1960s, which studied modes of thought from different perspectives, to various trends ("structural Marxism" and "political economy") in the 1970s that emphasized analysis of the nonnormative factors that shape the ways people behave. Ortner characterized the 1980s as a period in which there was an emphasis on modes of action. In this decade, anthropology focused on "practice," also referred to as "praxis, action, interaction, activity, experience, performance" (Ortner 1984:144; cf.127). This appears to confirm Firth's prediction of the rise of a "logistical" anthropology. Again, there is a pattern of alternation between levels of analysis, a shift that Firth describes (1975:8) as resulting from "a need for correction of interpretation by introducing new ways of looking at the phenomena."

These different styles of ethnography can be divided into two major categories. Structural and cultural (or symbolic) studies deal with modes of thought, and functional, processual, and logistical (or praxis) ethnographies deal with modes of action. Indeed, Ortner traces (1984:144, note 14) the recent emphasis on practice anthropology to the mode of action perspective embodied in the transactionalism of the 1950s and 1960s. Furthermore, Firth (1975:13) remarks that symbolic anthropology, with its emphasis on a people's "framework of ideas" and "mental map," is "congruent with what has formerly appeared as treatment of social structure or social norms," adding that this similarity makes it difficult to decide whether they reflect different modes of analysis or only a different way of talking about the same issues. Pocock (1961; cf. Dumont 1975) makes a similar point when he suggests that Evans-Pritchard's structural ethnography, *The Nuer* (1940a), marks a shift from "function to meaning," in effect a precursor of later symbolic or cultural analyses.

PLAN OF BOOK

It is by now apparent that understanding ethnographic texts requires paying careful attention to their levels of analysis and textual organization. Having indicated what these tasks involve, the remaining chapters illustrate them more fully by examining a few ethnographies in detail. By focusing on a limited number of cases, and by not trying to cover everything, I hope to gain a more careful and extended exploration of them, enabling me to make more clearly the central points about the nature of ethnographic argumentation. My goal is to provide a model of analysis, developed in the context of selected cases, that can be applied to still other ethnographies.

Let me add a word about the ethnographies chosen for examination. These illustrative cases (or exemplars) are drawn from among ethnographies that emphasize a modes of thought approach to social reality as well as from among those that focus on modes of action. I will also refer to ethnographic accounts that appear to mark a shift between them. I selected the particular cases because they are well known and clearly typify their theoretical presuppositions and styles of analysis. I expect that other anthropologists will have their own favorites and/or other preferences; I would hope that they would apply the model of reading ethnography presented herein to them, thereby evaluating its utility. It should also be noted that although most of the cases I discuss are standard realist ethnographies, I have included an example (Ortner's *Sherpas Through Their Rituals*) of what Marcus and Cushman (1982:25) have categorized as more recent experimental writing. Many of the experimental ethnographies identified by Marcus and Cushman were published at about the same time as Ortner's monograph and could have been used in place of it. It should be noted, however, that these experimental ethnographies are a mixed bag: some experiment with matters of textual organization, some with rhetorical style, and others with issues of reflexivity (for example, Rabinow's *Reflections on Fieldwork in Morocco* [1977], Dumont's *The Headman and I* [1978], and Favret-Saada's *Deadly Words: Witchcraft in the Bocage* [1977 in French and 1980 in English translation]).

Finally, I have not included for discussion in the main body of this book examples of reflexive ethnography, although I do address this style of writing in the concluding chapter. I have not done so because, as many anthropologists have noted (for example, Marcus and Cushman 1982:26, Roth 1989:559, Sangren 1988:564, Spencer 1989: 156–61), reflexive ethnographies have not (yet) contributed substantively to an explanation of a society or a culture, in contrast to the understanding they provide of the process and procedures by which anthropologists obtain their data. This should not be surprising since reflexive ethnographies are concerned with "techniques of discovery" rather than with "methods of validation" (cf. Spiro 1986:274).

There are at least two ways in which the remaining chapters could be arranged. One is to place the examples *chronologically*. Since the different modes of analysis salient in successive phases are a matter of "corrective emphasis," as Firth put it (1975:5), they could be presented in the order in which they were written. This choice would enable the reader to track changes in ethnographic focus as reactions to earlier works. The other is to group them in terms of their analytical foci, linking those that emphasize modes of thought or those that emphasize modes of action. This procedure directs attention to similarities of style and argumentation within these categories and also facilitates examining contrasts between them. I have chosen the latter approach.

The order of presentation is as follows. I begin with structural studies, using Evans-Pritchard's *The Nuer* (1940a) as a type case. I do so for two reasons. It is an eminent example of structural analysis, illustrating a modes of thought ethnography that focuses on material that is analytically prior to that contained in modes of action studies, in the sense that the study of modes of action implies antecedent modes of thought. It is also one of the first ethnographies intended to pose and resolve a theoretically defined problem, an orientation reflected in its elegant argument. It thus provides an excellent starting point for the examination of textual organization.

Next, I discuss several related symbolic studies, a style of ethnography resembling in many respects the earlier structural accounts. The examples of this type include an essay by Geertz (1973d) ("Deep Play") and a monograph, *Sherpas Through Their Rituals* (1978) by Ortner, a self-proclaimed "Geertzian" (Ortner 1984:129), which allows a fuller delineation of this mode of analysis.

Following these modes of thought analyses, I examine organizational ethnographies. The limitations of structural and symbolic ethnography are addressed in studies that focus on modes of action. I discuss the analytical framework that informs these accounts, drawing on concepts and strategies developed by Firth with regard to "social organization." I then describe several ethnographic monographs in which an "organizational" perspective was utilized to a lesser or greater degree: partially in Leach's *Political Systems of Highland Burma* (1954) and more fully in Barth's *Political Leadership among Swat Pathans* (1959) and Bailey's *Tribe, Caste, and Nation* (1960), although ethnographies written by other anthropologists trained at Manchester (for example, Mitchell 1956 or Turner 1957) could have been used as well.

In the next to last chapter, I compare different styles of ethnographic writing outlined above with respect to their uses of case materials and to the relationships they posit between procedures of discovery and those of presentation.

Finally, drawing on the ethnographic studies examined in preceding chapters, I consider their relevance to recent discussions concerning issues of rhetoric and reflexivity in ethnographic writing.

Chapter 2

STRUCTURAL ETHNOGRAPHY

Evans-Pritchard's *The Nuer* (1940a) is an anthropological classic and an excellent example of structural ethnography. In this chapter, I will discuss its argument, paying special attention to its textual organization, to the kinds of claims it contains, and to the kinds of data it presents in support of them. In doing so, I will review the monograph in detail, not only to illustrate a close reading of an ethnographic text but to establish a foundation for comparing different ethnographic accounts. For example, *The Nuer* describes a society in which the basis of social order is problematic. Other ethnographies, which will be examined in subsequent chapters, deal with similar questions but provide different solutions, differences that appear to be related in large part to the modes of analysis that characterize them.

Let me add a word about what I will not be doing. Since the goal of this chapter is to examine the way in which the monograph is constructed, I will not, for the most part, attempt to assess its claims by referring to arguments or evidence found outside this particular book. Therefore, I make little reference to the larger body of data available on the Nuer, much of it produced by Evans-Pritchard in two other monographs—*Kinship and Marriage Among The Nuer* (1951a) and *Nuer Religion* (1956)—and in a large number of essays (cf. the bibliographic information in Evans-Pritchard and Beidelman, 1971). Nor will I discuss the various reanalyses of Nuer tribal organization offered by other anthropologists (for example, Gluckman 1956, Sahlins 1961, Gough 1971, Southall 1976, Holy 1979, Karp and Maynard 1983, Kelly 1985, Meeker 1989), except to mention those that contain relevant data not included in Evans-Pritchard's monograph or enlarge upon themes that are suggested but undeveloped in *The Nuer*. In short, this chapter ana-lyzes *The Nuer*, but not the Nuer. It should be noted that in this chapter page numbers enclosed in parentheses, without a publication date, refer to this monograph.

THE PROBLEM OF THE NUER

What is the *The Nuer* about? At face value, according to its title and subtitle, the book is about a particular people, the Nuer, and specifically about their "modes of livelihood" and "political institutions." Its "theme," Evans-Pritchard states, is Nuer "political institutions" (4). It is also, we are told, a "description" (cf. the book's subtitle and p.3), a "plain account" (4) of the Nuer. It is, however, more than a simple description, a mere account of what is out there on the ground, since, as the ethnographer asserts repeated-ly, the goal of the monograph is to "understand" and "explain" Nuer behav-ior (cf. 4, 16, 19, 113, 119, 125, 132, 148, 181, and 235) *The Nuer* provides an interpretation of Nuer behavior.

What is it about Nuer "political institutions" that requires such under-standing and explanation? What is problematic or puzzling about the Nuer that requires interpretation? What, in other words, is the problem of the ethnography? It is not always easy for a reader to discern what question or set of questions underlies an ethnography, especially when beginning a read-ing of it. In *The Nuer*, however, Evans-Pritchard informs the reader, both directly and indirectly, about the aspect of Nuer life that has captured his interest. He writes of the "ordered anarchy" (6, 181) of the Nuer, an oxy-moron, which, by its seeming self-contradiction, flags the reader's attention. He also writes about the "remarkable" size of Nuer tribes (132), a word that indicates something unusual or extraordinary and worthy of attention. Both tribal size and the peculiar character of social order are noteworthy because the Nuer do not have obvious mechanisms of social control and political integration, at least in the eyes of one used to the governmental forms and political institutions of Western nation-states.

It is not merely the large size and wide distribution of Nuer tribes that call for explanation. If the Nuer were few in number, for example, in the hundreds or few thousands—similar to the size of Oceanic island popula-tions typically studied by anthropologists before Evans-Pritchard did field-work in the southern Sudan, or if they were distributed in small, isolated, and autonomous communities, as are the Anuak, as the ethnographer notes by way of comparison (119), or if they were not a proud, democratic, and bellicose people (48–50, 90, 151, 168–72, 235), then their "political order" (93, 118) might not be problematic. These conditions do prevail, however. [Moreover, the Nuer have interests that they pursue with great intensity and vigor and which, in conjunction with environmental constraints, force them into contact and potential conflict with one another thus necessitating some form of social control and social order.]

THE SOLUTION OF THE ETHNOGRAPHY

[Evans-Pritchard casts his answer to the question about social order among the Nuer in the form of a model of a segmentary system in which the constituent parts, local communities, are interrelated through a principle of balanced opposition.] The parts of the system are the "segments" or "sections" into which Nuer tribes are divided (139). The largest segments of a tribe are subdivided into smaller segments and these into even smaller segments. [In Evans-Pritchard's view, three levels of segmentation are sufficient to describe all Nuer tribes; the smallest tribal segment includes a number of local communities.] He describes tribal segments as being in a "structural equilibrium" (130, 147–48, 159) that is the product of a "structural principle" (142–43, 148). The principle, as Evans-Pritchard terms it, is a rule that specifies which segments will oppose one another or unite with one another in a process he calls "fission" and "fusion."]

These statements of the problem and the solution of the ethnography are a bare outline of Evans-Pritchard's argument. To appreciate its complexity and its subtlety, it is necessary to examine the order in which he presents it.

TEXTUAL ORGANIZATION

One of the great attractions of The Nuer is the elegance of its construction. Each chapter contributes to the formulation of its problem or to its solution. All the chapters are integrated to produce a coherent argument. (Some readers of The Nuer, however, argue a contrary view. Leach, for example, suggests that each part of the monograph is "autonomous and makes sense without reference to the rest" [1961:305]. Analysis of the textual organization of The Nuer, however, does not support Leach's position.) The account is divided into seven chapters, including an introduction and six substantive chapters, although, as indicated in the book's table of contents, the last chapter, dealing ostensibly with the age-set system of the

Nuer, contains Evans-Pritchard's summary and evaluation of the entire monograph. [It can be argued that the substantive chapters of the book are organized into three parts: the first two chapters ("Interest in Cattle" and "Oecology"); a middle chapter ("Time and Space"), which functions as a "bridge" between the parts; and the next two chapters ("The Political System" and "The Lineage System"), forming a linear and symmetrical "plan" (7, 249). The first part of the monograph sets the problem and begins to contribute to its resolution. The middle part moves the analysis from the constituent units of the political system (that is, local communities) to a conceptualization of relationships among them. The last part describes the rules that govern those relationships.]

There are several reasons to read *The Nuer* as tripartite in format. It is clear that the first two chapters are an integrated unit. [At the end of the chapter dealing with Nuer interest in cattle, Evans-Pritchard argues that cattle, in conjunction with the conditions required for their maintenance, lead to the necessity of tribal organization, yet those conditions are not described until the next chapter.] Moreover, he explicitly links the two chapters, arguing that "pastoral pursuits" and "environmental conditions" together contribute to the form of Nuer political structure (119, 261). It is also clear that the chapters on the political and lineage systems are integrated and that both are independent of that on the age-set system, which is not integral to the book's argument (cf. 190, 225, 260). Evans-Pritchard acknowledges that "it is easy to conceive of the political system existing without an age-set organization" (260). It appears that the chapter on age-sets, save its summary section, could be deleted from the book without weakening its principal conclusions.

[The first part of *The Nuer* functions to define the focal question of the ethnography. The first chapter ("Interest in Cattle") establishes that the Nuer have goals (the acquisition and possession of cattle) that they pursue with intensity and for which they are more than willing to fight.] It is this bellicosity that, in conjunction with Nuer patterns of mobility and contact (described in the second chapter), underlies the potential for disorder. Yet, Evans-Pritchard also uses this point to introduce into his account the proposition that the very same expectation—that people will fight over cattle—acts as a constraint on their actions and contributes to a modicum of social order.

[The second chapter (on "Oecology") develops further the interpretation of the problematic nature of Nuer social life.] Not only does the pursuit of their interests and their inclination to battle for them provide a motive for fighting, but their environment creates the opportunities for conflict. Evans-Pritchard establishes that the Nuer are "transhumant," moving from one part of their country to another in search of the resources necessary for the maintenance of their cattle and to engage in the other activities of their mixed economy. This mobility generates contact and therefore potential conflict among individuals and groups who are pursuing the same ends but who are not constrained by the sentiments and expectations arising from communal life.

⌐It is the combination of their disposition to fight—which Evans-Pritchard describes as their "aggressive impulses" and "predatory tendencies" (132)—and the necessity of their spatial mobility that creates the problem. Thus, the description of both their interests and their environment contributes to the argument that social life among the Nuer is problematic and that it requires a mechanism of social control for regulating relationships beyond the local group.⌐

⌐Evans-Pritchard also uses his account of Nuer ecology to define and describe local groups, the building blocks of their political system.⌐ Analyzing Nuer economic activities, he concludes that they suffer from a scarcity of food. He then argues that this insufficiency creates a direct interdependence among the members of local groups, both wet-season villages and dry-season camps, who have to rely upon one another for support in the struggle for survival. They are so drawn together that he treats them "as the smallest political groups in Nuerland" (85) Moreover, since the environmental conditions of Nuerland produce an indirect interdependence between persons dispersed over even wider areas, he concludes that the Nuer are compelled to accept "conventions of a political order" (93). Thus, Evans-Pritchard manages to establish in the first part of his argument that Nuer local communities are corporate units and that there must be rules governing behavior between such units.⌐

To move the argument from the level of depicting local groups to that of analyzing the system that contains them, Evans-Pritchard uses a bridging chapter ("Time and Space") to introduce Nuer concepts and norms about relationships. He focuses on the topics of time and space which imply relationships, those of sequence and of proximity. Moreover, he examines relationships as the Nuer understand them. For example, he begins this chapter with a description of Nuer terms for the divisions of an annual cycle, although he has already described, in the preceding chapter on ecology, seasons in Nuerland as a European would categorize them. After examining their temporal and spatial concepts, he concludes that Nuer conceive of them as a way of coordinating relationships rather than events, which he follows with a discussion of relationships between local communities.

Having introduced his concept of "structural distance" in discussing Nuer relationships, Evans-Pritchard then states his agenda for the rest of the ethnography: it is to discuss, in turn, the expression of such distance in the political, lineage, and age-set systems (113).

A close reading of the sequence of the analytical steps *within* the bridge chapter reveals the subtlety of the argument. Evans-Pritchard begins with a description of Nuer concepts of relationships. He then provides a "rough estimate" of Nuer population statistics. It may seem odd that he would introduce demographic data at this point in the argument (for example, it is the first time the reader is told how many Nuer there are), but it is logical, since he uses that material to get to a description of the local communities, villages (*cieng*) and camps (*wec*), in which the Nuer live. That places him in a position to describe the "values" that Nuer attach to these local communities, thereby introducing not only a categorization (albeit a "crude formal classification") of their social units, but also the sentiments and typical patterns of interaction associated with them. It is also here that he introduces the idea that "values are . . . embodied in words" (114). This directs attention to a change in the level of social reality to be analyzed and to the primary kind of data that will be utilized in that analysis. It also reaffirms that a Nuer village "is the political unit of Nuerland" (85, 115).

After describing the smallest political units of the Nuer, Evans-Pritchard shifts attention to the larger entities of which they are the constituent parts. Having argued that local communities combine into tribes, he then proceeds to enumerate these tribes and to define their characteristics, especially the sentiments and the moral rights and duties that their members share, including the distinguishing feature of the obligation to settle feuds and other disputes by arbitration. It is here that he introduces the distinction between "theory" and "practice" in reference to the discrepancy between the ways in which tribesmen should act and the ways in which they actually behave (120–21).

Evans-Pritchard uses the remaining sections of the chapter to place Nuer tribal organization in context and to comment on some methodological issues involved in the analysis he is attempting. He describes the defining characteristics of Nuer culture, contrasting them with those of neighboring peoples, and adds material on Nuer contacts with Arabs and Europeans in which the basic segmentary patterns of their internal relationships are replicated. In the last section of the chapter, Evans-Pritchard remarks on the difficulties of abstracting the meaning of Nuer terms, a significant problem given the emphasis on this procedure in his analysis.

To illustrate the problems of trying to understand behavior that is contextually variable, Evans-Pritchard interprets the Nuer word *cieng*, which he translates as "home." Because a person's identification of his home and his implied social identity may vary with circumstances (or with a changing reference point), and with it his or her rights and duties, or, in other words, the relevant rules of conduct, there may be a discrepancy between what people ought to do and what they do in fact. He argues, however, that although "political actualities are confused and conflicting ... [and are] not in accord with political values ... they tend to conform to them" (138). Moreover, he asserts in the final page of the chapter that behavior (or "actualities") can be understood only in relation to the moral obligations and normative rules (or "values") of the political system and its articulation with other systems of relationships. From this point, Evans-Pritchard moves to the third step of his argument: the analysis of Nuer political and lineage systems.

The chapter on the political system analyzes relationships between local groups. In it, Evans-Pritchard formulates his principle of segmentation to explain tribal fission and fusion and analyzes the apparently paradoxical role of the feud in maintaining tribal solidarity. He proceeds first, as I have indicated earlier, by asserting that tribes are divided into "segments" (or "sections") and then by defining their characteristics. Having posited the existence of tribes and tribal segments, he then argues that they oppose and combine with one another according to what he describes as a "segmentary principle," the rule specifying which units, under which conditions, will become either allies or enemies.

Fighting provides the occasions for these shifting alliances, but fights occur more frequently within a Nuer tribe than between Nuer tribes. This happens because segments within a tribe, as local and contiguous communities, have more contacts with one another than with segments of other tribes and thus have more opportunities to come into conflict. Therefore, there must be a mechanism that permits members of tribal segments to resolve their disputes, so that they may get on with the routine tasks of daily life and so that they may coalesce with one another in forming a unit in intertribal warfare. Evans-Pritchard argues that feuding is the institution that affords a degree of tribal cohesiveness, and he uses the remaining sections of the chapter to describe, at a theoretical level, the conventions of fighting and of settling feuds. Furthermore, since the resolution of a feud, however temporary, involves the participation of leopard-skin chiefs, he also uses this discussion of feuds as a point of departure for commenting on such chiefs and other men influential in local communities.

From an account of the political system, Evans-Pritchard goes on to analyze lineage relationships. There are two major reasons to describe the lineage system of the Nuer and to place discussion of it after that of the political system. The first is that the Nuer speak of territorial groups in lineage terms: "territorial affiliation" is expressed in a "lineage idiom" (205). Therefore, to understand local groups and their relationships, Evans-Pritchard proceeds to analyze the lineage system. The other reason for analyzing the lineage system is that it provides a structural framework, a "conceptual skeleton" (212), for the political system, which is composed of local communities.

Evans-Pritchard then advances his argument by exploring the ways in which the lineage system constitutes a conceptual skeleton for Nuer territorial groups. He develops the argument systematically: lineages are not localized; each local community is associated with a segment of a lineage that is dominant in a tribal area; therefore, the lineage system facilitates integration between local groups, since it is dispersed over a wide area. More importantly, the lineage system, unlike the tribal system, provides for continuity in the relationships between local groups, because tribal membership is transient and lineage membership is permanent. Several causes of lineage dispersion are described: intralineage fighting, migration, and, connected to a pastoral way of life, little attachment to particular localities (209). (Evans-Pritchard's discussion of the causes of Nuer dispersal reveals an apparent contradiction in his interpretation. On the one hand, he argues that the Nuer as pastoralists do not feel tied to any particular spot, a conclusion further supported by his observation that the Nuer do not have an organized cult of ancestral ghosts nor sacred places associated with them [209–10]. On the other hand, in his argument that they have tribal sentiments, he asserts that a Nuer is so attached to his place of birth that he performs a ritual to break the "mystical ties" that bind him to it and to "build up" those with his new place of residence [120].) Although Nuer may move from one place to another, thereby changing tribal identity (it is a function of where a person resides), they cannot change lineage identity (210, 213).

The persistence of lineage membership reveals the logic of Evans-Pritchard's decision to describe first the political system and then the lineage system. Membership in a local community primarily determines one's loyalties and obligations, particularly in fighting and in forming alliances, but such commitments are subject to change. Their political system organizes the daily life of the Nuer, but it is potentially unstable. The lineage system, however, represents enduring social identities and therefore continuity in the relationships between local groups. If the Nuer could change lineage identities as readily as they can change place of residence, there would be no basis for conceptual consistency and no mechanism for organizing tribes.

CLAIMS

In the introductory chapter, I discussed anthropological analyses and the ethnographies that derive from them, indicating that they may be classified in terms of the kind of social reality that they describe or to which they refer. And so the question: At what level of analysis does Evans-Pritchard interpret Nuer social order? That is, does he offer an account in terms of what Nuer think (their concepts and norms), or in terms of what Nuer do (their actions), or in terms of the relationships between them? Another way of posing this question is to ask about the kinds of claims being made in the ethnography.

In the case of *The Nuer* the answer is complicated. It contains accounts of what Nuer do *and* of what they think. These descriptions, how-ever, refer to different aspects of Nuer life. In only one part of the mono-graph are they treated together. For example, in identifying and isolating Nuer local communities, Evans-Pritchard writes of both Nuer attitudes and actions. In writing of relationships between such local groups, however, he focuses almost entirely on Nuer ideas. Indeed, it is his emphasis on Nuer concepts about relationships, which he describes as a "different order of real-ity" (94) from that of local groups, that justifies classifying *The Nuer* as an example of structural ethnography.

Evans-Pritchard's emphasis on Nuer notions is reflected in both what he explicitly describes as the innovative and theoretically significant contri-bution of *The Nuer* (261–66) and in the amount of attention he gives to their analysis in chapters 3–6—almost 70 percent of the monograph, more than twice the space allocated to the analysis of the nature of local commu-nities in chapters 1 and 2. This emphasis on systems of thought is also con-sistent with Evans-Pritchard's use of verbal data to support his claims about Nuer concepts, moral obligations, and normative rules. It may be disconcert-ing, however, to a reader who is led, by the ethnographer's statements about his methods of doing fieldwork, to expect primarily an account of what Nuer do. For example, he remarks that his account is largely based on "direct observation" (9, 15), although he acknowledges that he did not see much of what he describes (152, 163–64, 185).

In seeking "understanding" and "explanation" of Nuer political insti-tutions, Evans-Pritchard focuses on normative rules that are said to govern Nuer behavior. He derives them from various analytical units: "customs," "values," "conventions," and "concepts." His interest in what people ought to do, with how they should behave, rather than with their actual behavior, is also evident in the distinction he draws between Nuer behavior in "theo-ry" and in "practice" and in the stress he places on the former.

Evans-Pritchard's emphasis on normative rules in describing Nuer trib-al organization contrasts with the use he makes of historical evidence in sup-port of his interpretation of relationships between Nuer and others. Thus, he refers to traveler's reports in describing relationships between Nuer and Dinka and between Nuer and strangers (126–27; 132–35). That is, his nor-mative ahistorical approach to the analysis of Nuer tribal organization differs from his reference to historical events in the analysis of extratribal action.

From the beginning of his account, Evans-Pritchard indicates that "customs" are the units of his analysis. He declares that, at the end of his first period of fieldwork among the Nuer, he "had learnt a little of the language but had the scantiest notes of their customs" (11) and, in describing the difficulties of working among the Nuer, he punned about the technique by which they blocked his questions about their "customs" (12; cf. 1, 3, 14, 17, 18, 83, and 128). Although "custom" is not defined in The Nuer, it is apparent from his references that it has a normative dimension, for example, "people ought not to kill an ox solely for food" (26).

It is in the analysis of Nuer "values" that the structural character of the ethnography is more obvious. Evans-Pritchard uses the word "value" in at least two different ways. In the first part of the ethnography, dealing with Nuer interests in cattle, he depicts values in terms of economic utility and cultural ends, the pursuit of which motivates the Nuer. In the rest of the argument, however, he uses the term to refer to normative rules and their role in restraining conduct, the means by which social order is achieved. Thus, he defines political values as " . . . the common feeling and acknowl edgement of members of local communities that they are an exclusive group distinct from, and opposed to, other communities of the same order, and that they ought to act together in certain circumstances and to observe certain conventions among themselves" (263; cf. 5, 115, 119–22). More succinctly, values are "sentiments" and "norms" (228). He pays some attention to the affective or psychological dimension of values in governing relationships (90, 120, 123, 152, 181–84), but the major part of his argument turns on their normative aspect.

Elsewhere in a condensation of his argument about the Nuer tribal system, Evans-Pritchard omits mention of sentiments altogether and defines a tribe simply in terms of the moral obligations to settle disputes by arbitration and to combine in warfare against other similar units and against foreigners (cf. 1940b:278). In his interpretation of "values" as normative rules, he follows Durkheim's analysis of "social facts" (cf. Durkheim 1938 [1895]). Indeed, a comparison of the argument of The Nuer with Durkheim's analyses of the role of customs, moral obligations and normative rules in structuring and in understanding social life reveals the intellectual tradition from which it derives.

This is evident in the definition of a "tribe." Fellow tribesmen have a "common sentiment" toward one another (119, 122) and various "moral obligations" (122), including those of uniting in war and settling feuds by arbitration (122). In discussing these moral obligations, described as "formal" characteristics (148), Evans-Pritchard uses the terms "duties" and "conventions" (119–21), implying the idea of rules and standards. Indeed, he alludes to different kinds of "rules" in Nuer life: those of war (146), of settling a feud (175), and of exogamy (225).

The idea that "conventions" structure Nuer life is central to the argument of *The Nuer*. Evans-Pritchard argues that the potential for "continuous turmoil" among the Nuer, as they seek to satisfy their interests in cattle, is constrained by a "recognition of conventions in the settlement of disputes," conventions that he equates with "tribal organization" (50, 93). Moreover, he distinguishes between actions and conventions, suggesting that the former are under the control or influence of the latter: "Fighting between Nuer of different tribes was . . . subject to certain conventions . . . " (121).

That Evans-Pritchard is analyzing the normative aspects of social reality is also evident in his discussion of Nuer concepts. He asserts that concepts imply values and that "values . . . are embodied in words" (114), thereby linking Nuer concepts with their words and both with their values (203). Moreover, the concepts (and the normative rules that they imply) that concern him are those shared among the Nuer and whose meaning is social and public: they are collective representations. Richards commented on this aspect of Evans-Pritchard's analysis in her review of the book. She wrote that the "chapter on Nuer concepts of time and space is one of the most brilliant in the book. Here for the first time Durkheim's stimulating treatment of time and space as 'collective representations' . . . is worked out in concrete detail" (1941:46). Thus, in discussing "structural" time, Evans-Pritchard examines only Nuer concepts that are collectively defined (104), excluding from consideration "the way in which an individual perceives time" (107).

Similarly, he is concerned only with behavior that corresponds with Nuer terms. Behavior that is not conceptualized by the Nuer, as evident in their cultural categories, is not included in his analysis of tribal organization. For example, he examines social units that are embodied in Nuer "socio-spatial categories" (114), especially the local communities of *cieng* and *wec*, "village" and "camp." He excludes from analysis, however, the unit that he describes as a "district" (116), a group of local communities in which people have easy and frequent contact, because it is not conceptualized by the Nuer (124–25, 226) and does not constitute a Nuer "category" (116). Again, it is clear that Evans-Pritchard is primarily interested in Nuer ideas. He is concerned with their behavior, but only to the extent to which it is a product of their collective representations and consistent with their social categorization.

The distinction Evans-Pritchard draws between the "theory" and "practice" of Nuer behavior represents additional evidence that *The Nuer* is a structural analysis, focusing on modes of thought. Thus, in discussing tribal rights and duties, he notes that how people should behave "in theory" contrasts with how they behave "in practice" (120–21; 143, 164, 169). He makes the same point when he contrasts "values" with "actualities": "actualities . . . are not always, even in a political context, in accord with political values, though they tend to conform to them" (138; 263–64). The contrasts between theory and practice (and between values and actualities) parallels the difference between the "formal definition" of a tribe and what happens "in fact" (148, 149). Thus, one set of terms ("theory," "value," "convention," "rule," and "formal definition") contrasts with another set of terms ("practice," "actualities," and "fact"), each indicating the different levels of social reality that they represent. It is also clear that The Nuer is aimed at understanding Nuer behavior "in theory," that is, in terms of how they ought to behave rather than in terms of how they actually behave.

DATA

The different kinds of claims contained in The Nuer call for different kinds of evidence. In support of his claims about Nuer local communities and the conditions that lead to their existence, Evans-Pritchard introduces linguistic, behavioral, and visual evidence. For example, he asserts that "cattle are the superlative value of Nuer life" (48), supporting this claim with Nuer statements about, as well as his own observations of, Nuer cattle-keeping practices (21–26; 31–36), of their uses of cattle for food (26–28) and other by-products (28–31). He also introduces Nuer cattle terms (41–45), including a diagrammatic representation of the color patterns of Nuer cattle, and Nuer songs (46–47) as evidence for his conclusion.

He is explicit about his reasons for introducing verbal evidence in this context:

> Linguistic profusion in particular departments of life is one of the signs by which one quickly judges the direction and strengths of a people's interests. It is for that reason, rather than for its intrinsic importance, that we draw the reader's attention to the volume and variety of the Nuer cattle vocabulary (41).

He also asserts that cattle are of great psychological significance to the Nuer (40). Although he presents no data directly revealing Nuer mental and emotional states, he offers as illustration of the "identification of man with cattle" (41) a number of drawings (Figures 7 and 13) and photographs (the Frontispiece and Plates III, V, and XVII), because they "present a classic picture of savagery" and "convey to [the reader] better than I can do in words the crudity of kraal life" (40).

In support of his conclusions about the ways in which ecological constraints shape Nuer communities, Evans-Pritchard relies primarily on visual data, his own observations, and those of other foreigners, giving little or no attention to what Nuer say about the matter. Thus, in writing about seasonal variations, he draws on government records about temperature and rainfall (52) and his own assessments about the times of the year that Nuer spend in villages and camps (57–63). (This contrasts notably with his discussion of Nuer concepts of seasons and the movements they associate with them.) He describes the grasses that feed Nuer herds and the soil and water conditions on which these depend. He also uses government photographs to depict Nuerland as a "dead level plain" (53; Plates VI, XIa and b, and XIXb). For evidence of Nuer transhumant movements, he presents sketch maps (56, 58, 60) of the directions in which tribal sections travel, one of which is based on information that presumably he collected, although the others are based on information provided by English colonial officers and others associated with the Nuer (x).

To establish the corporate character of local groups, Evans-Pritchard provides evidence that they are localized settlements and that their members are dependent on one another. He presents photographs (Plates VIIa and b, VIII, XII, XVa, XVI, XVII, XVIII, XIXa and XXIb), including one air-view taken by the Royal Air Force, showing particular villages and camps, their sites, and the modes of construction used in them. He estimates Nuer food production and consumption, based on his own observations and those of other Europeans (71, and Plates IX, X, XXIIa and b) as well as on Nuer stories and myths about food preferences and periods of hunger (81–83). In concluding that food scarcity leads the Nuer, in a display of social solidarity, to share food (84), he depends on his observations of food consumption and food exchange between people of different households within a local community as well as on his analysis of Nuer rules of hospitality and conventions about the division of food (84–85).

Although he does not give specific information about whom he observed eating or sharing food with others or where and when such sharing took place, he does claim that it happens to such an extent, that, "looked at from outside, the whole community is seen to be partaking of a joint supply" (84). Moreover, he states the logic underlying this behavior: it makes sense when people have to pool their resources to cope with the common experience of deprivation, "for it is scarcity and not sufficiency that makes people generous, since everybody is thereby insured against hunger" (85).

Evans-Pritchard also depicts Nuer material culture in order to support his contention that local communities are solidary and the building blocks of their political system. He uses photographs (Frontispiece and Plates VIII and XXIX) and figures (Figures 3, 4, 11, 12, and 14) to argue that with few and simple material objects, trade and exchange between settlements is limited, a limitation that further underlines the interdependence within local communities. He uses figures and photographs as evidence to support his claims about Nuer material culture rather than describing it in words (85).

His characterization, then, of villages and camps as corporate communities is based on observed and reported activities within them and on his inference of the logic that appears to underlie these activities. His decision to treat these communities as the "smallest political groups in Nuerland" (85) follows from his analysis of their internal relationships and not from his observation of intervillage relationships.

[Evans-Pritchard's use of visual materials is particularly striking.] He presents photographs and drawings as evidence of the value of cattle to Nuer and of their local communities. [Seventy-five per cent of the photographs contained in the book (thirty of the forty-one) refer to the description of local communities. (The other eleven photos depict individual Nuer.) All the figures, no matter where they occur in the book, refer to Nuer "interests" and local groups.] It is important to note these visual materials are distributed throughout the monograph, although they refer only to claims made in the first two chapters of the ethnography. That they are scattered throughout the book and are included within the chapters on the abstract relationships that constitute the political and lineage systems may lead the reader to conclude that these "systems" are characterized by a concreteness comparable to that demonstrated for Nuer interests in cattle and for their local communities. Interpretations about relationships between local communities, that is, about the political system, however, are based on other kinds of evidence.

Evans-Pritchard describes relationships between local communities in terms of the "values" or normative rules that are supposed to govern conduct between their members and he derives these rules from verbal data. Verbal data are used as evidence for such relationships because, as he asserts, "values . . . are embodied in words" (114). Thus, the evidence for claims about tribal organization consists of Nuer concepts and Nuer statements about how they should behave.

The analysis of tribal rights and duties illustrates his use of this sort of data. He asserts that a primary characteristic of a tribe is the expectation of compensation for homicide committed against fellow tribesmen (5, 120–21, 152–62). As evidence he introduces a number of Nuer terms. Thus, he analyzes Nuer concepts for different kinds of fighting, among which there is *kur*, a generic term for fighting and the word for intertribal fighting, and *ter*, which refers to intratribal fighting. He also states that the Nuer have a concept, *cut*, that refers to wealth to be paid in compensation for killing a member of one's own tribe.

In unpacking of the meaning of these terms, he expounds upon the normative rules that define a tribe. Thus, the difference between *kur* and *ter*, inter- and intratribal fighting, is related to the way Nuer deal with homicides that may result from fighting. A homicide's kinsmen are obliged to seek vengeance for their murdered relative. Moreover, their neighbors become involved in seeking revenge, because of the norms regarding their relationships with one another. This could lead to a feud, a lengthy and continuing hostility between local communities. Within a tribe, however, there is the feeling that compensation through the payment of bloodwealth (*cut*) can and should be paid in order to resolve the conflict. Such compensation, and therefore the possibility of settling feuds, is neither expected nor acknowledged for a homicide involving members of different tribes.

Evans-Pritchard's description of the rules for settling a feud provides another example of his use of verbal data. Thus, he writes that the murderer (*gwan thunga*) goes to the home of a ritual specialist, a "leopard-skin chief" (*kuaar muon*), to seek asylum during which time his relatives negotiate the payment of compensation to the victim's relatives. The ritual specialist acts as a mediator, ascertaining what the murderer's people (*jithunga*) are able and willing to pay to the dead man's people (*jiran*). "In theory," a number of cattle are paid and cleansing sacrifices are performed. Even then, however, the potential for conflict persists, since the threat of renewed killings exists because of the feelings aroused in the kinsmen of the slayer and the slain. As evidence for these sentiments, Evans-Pritchard presents his translations of Nuer proverbs and maxims: for example, "A bone (the dead man) lies between them" (154, 155).

Verbal data, then, constitutes the evidence for the claims about cultural categories and normative rules. Throughout the book, Evans-Pritchard refers to what Nuer "declare," "hold," "say," or "told" him (22, 23, 26, 35, 49, 84, 120, 121, 127, 143, 156, 157, 167, 175, 176, 209, 217, 221). In addition to their statements, he presents and analyzes their concepts. He uses Nuer statements and concepts as an indicator of what they know, believe, and feel.

EVALUATING THE ARGUMENT

It is evident that *The Nuer* has several strengths. In addition to the "elegance" and "beautiful lucidity" of Evans-Pritchard's ethnography, attested to by several anthropologists, including those who disagree with his interpretation (Leach 1954:283; 1961:5, 304), it has other features to commend it. It is a model of argumentation. In Evans-Pritchard's own assessment, *The Nuer* represents a contribution to anthropological theory and to the presentation of ethnographic facts in relation to theoretical issues. He argues that he has "subordinated" description to analysis precisely because he believes that anthropological theory is to be advanced by describing "facts in relation to a theory of them and as exemplifications of it" (261).

Several anthropologists have commented on the scarcity of ethnographic data in *The Nuer* (for example, Richards 1941, Kaberry 1957, Leach

1954, 1961). Evans-Pritchard argues that it is an advance to include in an ethnography only those facts that are "significant" to a theoretical point of view (261). While it may be argued that this strategy generates an ethnography different from those "lengthy monographs . . . [which] generally record observations in too haphazard a fashion to be either pleasant or profitable" (261), it also raises the issue of whether the facts support the theory or the theory illuminates the facts, and whether there may be alternative interpretations of the same set of recorded facts.

The Nuer depicts a system of moral obligations and normative rules in terms of which action is intelligible. Evans-Pritchard states several reasons for undertaking this task. First, what people actually do is difficult to understand: "actualities are confused and conflicting" (138). Second, values, customs, and conventions direct, control, and regulate behavior (211, 225), or at least behavior tends to conform to normative rules (138, 264). And, finally, what people do can be understood only when seen in relation to their ideas about what should be done (138).

He reinforces his analysis of Nuer rules—the informal logic of their system—by examining mechanisms that permit variations in actualities while the rules remain constant. Thus, he describes the contextual variation of meaning and the related notion of the plasticity of Nuer concepts. The different meanings of a concept are evident in his analysis of the multiple referents of social categories such as "home" (136). Another example of the flexibility of Nuer rules of tribal organization is evident in his analysis of the ways in which they are bent in response to socio-demographic changes. He explains how normative rules can be made to accommodate such changes, thereby maintaining the system. He describes several procedures (222–28) that, in accord with the size of the population in question, permit new members to be incorporated into the political system through affiliation with a lineage: by adoption, by the assimilation of cognatic to agnatic ties, and by the "mythological creation of kinship fictions."

Thus, Evans-Pritchard's account of the way Dinka and other strangers "become Nuer" (caa Nath) or "become a member of the community" (caa dil e cieng or caa ran wec) illustrates a mechanism by which a person (or group of persons) with one social identity takes on another, allowing the rules that define the system to be adapted to ecological and economic changes and to the consequences of feuds and warfare. That is, he analyzes the ways in which the lineage system persists despite changes in social life which might otherwise disrupt or threaten it.

If these features of The Nuer are among its strong points, they are counterbalanced by several weaknesses. Evans-Pritchard fails to provide evidence critical for his argument and overlooks the importance of data contrary to it; and he misses opportunities to develop alternative models relevant to his interpretation of Nuer tribal organization and to his more general strategy of understanding behavior.]

One of the major problems with the evidence presented in *The Nuer* concerns the data that Evans-Pritchard provides about the problem of the ethnography. For example, he presents very little evidence to support his claims about the problematic nature of Nuer tribal organization. He asserts that order is maintained over wide areas (50, 113, 132, 181). Yet it is questionable over how wide an area such maintenance of order exists, since he also claims that interaction, both cooperation and conflict, takes place within narrow territorial limits (137–38, 142, 149–50, 157, 162).

There is also little evidence in *The Nuer* to support Evans-Pritchard's claims about the existence of tribes. For example, he provides no Nuer word for "tribe." In classifying Nuer "socio-spatial categories" (114), he presents Nuer terms for local groups ranging from a hut (*dwil* or *ut*) to a village (*cieng*) or camp (*wec*), but offers no evidence that the Nuer have a term for larger collectivities. This is particularly troublesome for an interpretation that is based on translation and systematization of Nuer concepts as "embodied in words." He does state that every "tribe has a name which refers to its members and to their country (*rol*)" (119), but that name may refer to a lineage (or to one of its segments) or to a geographical area (194). In addition, Nuer ordinarily use their terms for "home" (*cieng*) or "lineage" (*thok dwiel*) to identify themselves (195, 204).

The status of clan is similar. He tells us that "a clan is not to Nuer an abstraction and there is no word in their language that can be translated 'clan' in ours" (195). Thus, of "village," "lineage," "tribe," and "clan," the primary units of his analysis of the political system, only the terms for local communities are translations of Nuer words.

Moreover, there is a discrepancy between his conceptualization of tribal units and that of the Nuer. He defines a tribe in terms of rights and duties that are recognized between individuals. For example, he argues that tribal boundaries may be drawn according to the obligation to pay and accept bloodwealth in compensation for homicide. Using that criterion, he distinguishes between two tribes, whereas the Nuer recognize a single community. He abstracts a "tribe" from Nuer statements indicating whether or not they hold a normative rule in common and not because there is a term that corresponds to a "structural" unit as reflected in their terminology. This is inconsistent with his pronounced methodology for analyzing Nuer concepts.

Thus, it appears that his claims about tribes follow from his analytical distinctions. He implies the existence of a tribe by describing its component parts. For example, he outlines the features of local groups (villages and camps) and then, having established their existence, presents a list of tribes that are more inclusive units. Similarly, he begins his analysis of the political system with an account of the characteristics of local groups, which he defines as tribal segments, implying the existence of a larger entity. That is, he posits the existence of Nuer tribes and describes the characteristics of their constituent parts (various local groupings), which then becomes the evidence for his claims about Nuer tribes. It is possible that local groups have the features that Evans-Pritchard attributes to them; it does not necessarily follow that such local groups constitute (or combine to form) larger, more inclusive entities.

That the data Evans-Pritchard uses do not necessarily establish the existence of tribes is also evident in his discussion of fighting. He mentions two kinds of fighting recognized by Nuer and reflected in their words, ter and kur. He argues that they refer to intratribal and intertribal fighting respectively, thus supporting, by implication, his contention that there are tribes. On the other hand, these terms could simply differentiate between fighting within and between lineages or between fighting for which compensation should or should not be paid, a difference primarily between fighting within local communities and fighting outside them. In any case, the types of fighting indicate the corporate nature of local communities. They are not evidence for the existence of the tribes. Incidentally, ter is not translated as "feud" fighting, but rather as a fight for which there is the possibility of arbitration and compensation.

There is also little evidence that Nuer act tribally, although Evans-Pritchard suggests that they do. For example, he writes that "in 1927, the Nuong tribe killed their District Commissioner, while at the same time the Lou openly defied the Government and the Gaawar attacked Duk Faiyuil Police Post" (135). This may suggest that tribes acted corporately, but it is not evident from his account just how many of the estimated 9,000 Nuong, 34,000 Lou, or 20,000 Gaawar took part in these "tribal" actions. Indeed, in an analysis of the origins of the biased image of the Nuer held by explorers, administrators, and ethnographers, Johnson describes what actually happened in this case:

> After the decision to campaign against Guek [a Nuer prophet] and the Lou had already been taken in 1927, Captain V.H. Fergusson, District Commissioner of the Western Nuer in Bahr al-Ghazal Province, was murdered by two Nyuong Nuer. It was at first assumed that this murder was instigated by a Nyuong Nuer prophet, and Willis [a colonial administrator] used this as further proof of the subversive character of prophets. It was only after both the murderers were captured and tried that it was learned that a seemingly 'loyal' government chief with a personal grudge against Fergusson had instigated the murder and then circulated rumours blaming the prophet... (1981:523–24, n.12).

Thus, the evidence for the solution to the ethnographic puzzle is weak and inconclusive. The argument that Nuer conceive of or act in terms of a segmentary principle is not a strong one. Evans-Pritchard concludes that maintenance of order at the extralocal level is the product of a segmentary system in which local communities combine with one another into larger segments when threatened by segments of the same order of inclusiveness. He argues that Nuer state this segmentary principle in describing who would fight against whom. On the other hand, he acknowledges that the process of unification and the "pattern of combinations were not always as regular and simple as they were explained to me and as I have stated them" (144).

Moreover, *The Nuer* includes data that do not support Evans-Pritchard's segmentary model. For example, in the few cases of tribal conflicts that he uses to illustrate the operation of the segmentary principle (144–46), the alliances actually formed are not in accord with it. In the segmentary model, the normative rule is that "members of any segment unite for war against adjacent segments of the same order and unite with these adjacent segments against larger sections" (142). In kinship terms, this would mean that brothers would unite against first cousins, first cousins would unite against second cousins, and so on; and that agnates would unite against affines, for example, brothers against maternal nephews, and so on. That is the theory. In the examples presented, two groups, related as mother's brother and sister's son, joined together in opposition to a group related as a brother to one of those groups, which contradicts the segmentary principle.

Furthermore, Evans-Pritchard's own analysis suggests other ways of interpreting Nuer social order. He indicates that in *practice* "political cohesion" varies with the size of the local group (137–38, 142, 149–50, 156, 157, 159, 162, 169). That is, the smaller the local group, the more cohesive it is; and conversely, the larger the local group, the less cohesive it is. This principle holds because the costs of resolving hostilities (or failing to resolve them) varies with the distance between those in conflict. The hypothesis is not part of Evans-Pritchard's structural model: it is not abstracted from Nuer concepts nor from a systematization of Nuer moral obligations. Rather it states the conditions under which such obligations are likely to be honored. The ethnographer formulates this principle; it is based on his analysis of the relationship between normative rules and the costs of implementing them. As such, it differs from the rules "embodied in words." This alternative explanation foreshadows what later came to be called an "organizational" approach to ethnography, yet is neither developed nor emphasized in the argument of *The Nuer*.

Another interpretation, related to the preceding one, is also indicated by Evans-Pritchard. For example, he notes that social order obtains between people who reside close to one another because the resolution of conflict is a necessity for daily life (156). Conflict is dampened because individual Nuer have allegiances to two kinds of groups, local communities and lineages, which are not mutually exclusive. That is, a man might have to fight on behalf of his neighbors and against his kinsmen, since not all of his relatives live in his village. Such conflicts of loyalties tend to limit hostilities, leading more readily to their quick and effective resolution. Although Evans-Pritchard did not develop this line of argument, Gluckman (1956) did elaborate upon it.

The level of analysis at which Evans-Pritchard constructs his interpretation precludes him from analyzing processual issues such as the dynamics of political leadership among the Nuer, although his own data are relevant to them. He asserts that a "village is a political unit in a structural sense, but it has no political organization" (180). This conclusion leads him to overlook the ways in which influential men (a "bull" or a *tut* in Nuer usage) build up and maintain a following. While recording the qualifications of these local leaders and noting the transactions through which they "gain a social reputation" (179–80), he does not explore the implications of these observations for an understanding of Nuer political organization. For example, a "bull" gathers around him a following of kinsmen (179), and it is stated that a man can get the compensation owed to him only if his kinsmen back him (162, 167, 169). Furthermore, since a man attracts followers by entertaining them and by providing them with cattle for bridewealth, he must have sufficient animals to enable him to act accordingly. Since one of the ways in which a Nuer acquires such property is through fighting, it follows that a leader may be one who is particularly successful at raiding and stealing others' cattle. It also follows that such fighting is likely to generate feuds, and thus feuding may represent the outcome of efforts to gain political influence. Although Evans-Pritchard does not pursue this sort of argument, Barth (1959) develops it in a monograph (to be discussed in Chapter Four) that emphasizes a modes of action approach to ethnography.

Finally, Evans-Pritchard's focus on normative rules and his assumption that behavior tends to conform to them leads him to ignore choices that individuals can make in selecting a course of action. Some choices are implied in his analyses of the conditions under which social control is likely to be effective. That is, to hypothesize that people do not attempt to enforce a settlement if the costs of doing so are too great suggests that they have alternatives between which they choose according to some calculation of their best interests. Choice is also implied in the analysis of the situational selection of social identities. That is, an individual can choose to regard himself (or another) as a member of one or another tribal or lineage segment, and, by selecting one rather than another identity, he shapes the interaction that follows from such a decision (135–38, 147–48, 195, 198).

Moreover, the selection of a place of residence is not fixed, but allows of alternatives among which an individual can choose, and more than once at that. For example, individuals can and do move from one village to another to avoid disputes, to improve their economic prospects, or simply because they are restless (65, 209–10). Whether they choose to move or to remain in a particular village, and to which village they decide to go, are choices that influence Nuer tribal organization, because they reflect and cause not only changes in political alliances but also in patterns of conflicting loyalties and thus political cohesion among the Nuer.

[Examination of choice, or of the "optative element" as it has come to be known, does not characterize structural ethnographies such as *The Nuer*. Rather, they typically represent efforts to discern and to describe the standards in terms of which such choices are (or should be) made.]That is, in ethnography that focuses on systems of thought, standards (or values or normative rules) are taken as problematic, and the alternative courses of action receive less systematic attention.[In modes of action ethnographies, the emphasis shifts to a concern with the processes by which social forms come into being and are maintained and to social change as a product of the interaction between standards and alternatives for choice.]

Chapter 3

SYMBOLIC ETHNOGRAPHY

In the preceding chapter, I discussed a style of ethnography as it appeared in a seminal monograph published in 1940. In this chapter, I turn to another style, usually described as symbolic or interpretive ethnography, which characterizes many contemporary accounts. In several ways, symbolic ethnographies resemble structural studies. Like structural studies, they focus on the meaning of behavior and rely primarily on verbal data in support of their interpretations. Indeed, in this respect, they are sufficiently similar that it is not inaccurate to describe symbolic ethnographies as neostructural in style.

A MODEL OF SYMBOLIC ETHNOGRAPHY: "DEEP PLAY"

Clifford Geertz is a leading practitioner of symbolic ethnography and many of the most interesting examples of it are found among his essays in *The Interpretation of Cultures* (1973a). In "Thick Description: Toward an Interpretive Theory of Culture" (1973b), he argues that the aim of anthropology is to interpret the meaning of behavior, to explain actions and attitudes that appear puzzling (cf. 1973b:5, 16). This task is accomplished by depicting behavior in terms of the culture in which it occurs. Culture, in

49

this sense, [as Geertz describes it, consists of "structures of signification," "frames of interpretation," or "socially established structures of meaning" (1973b:9, 12), by reference to which people act and interact with one another and interpret their own behavior as well as that of others. For Geertz, then, culture is a "context" (1973b:14), and the object of ethnography is to describe it, revealing the premises and assumptions on which the "informal logic" of behavior is based.]

This emphasis on modes of thought and meaning in symbolic ethnography is evident in Geertz's interpretation of the Balinese cockfight, "Deep Play: Notes on the Balinese Cockfight" (1973d). For Geertz, the cockfight is a symbolic event which offers a window into Balinese culture, through which it is possible to see "what being a Balinese 'is really like'" (1973d:417). He interprets the event as a cultural form, a "text," through which one attempts to understand the "inner nature" of Balinese society (1973d:417).

Geertz attributes two meanings to the cockfight. On the one hand, he argues that it has a sociological function, contributing to the maintenance of social order. However, he also claims that more significant is its interpretive function: "it is a Balinese reading of Balinese experience, a story they tell themselves about themselves" (1973d:448). This cultural form constitutes for the Balinese a model of themselves and of their society.]

But, Geertz continues, the cockfight does something else as well. It not only expresses social reality in such a way so as to make it comprehensible to the Balinese, it also transforms them. That is, the cockfight, as a text, as an art form, works by shaping the minds of those who experience it. As Geertz puts it, "Attending cockfights and participating in them is, for the Balinese, a kind of sentimental education" (1973d:449). Repeated exposure to this event is the means by which the cockfight works its transformation. As Geertz states: "Enacted and reenacted . . . the cockfight enables the Balinese . . . to see a dimension of his own subjectivity," adding that "cockfights . . . are positive agents in the creation and maintenance of such a sensibility" (1973d:450–51). The cockfight embodies a worldview and informs men about it. It is explanatory; it is instructive. Thus, the cockfight, as a symbolic event, is not only a window into Balinese culture (for the Balinese as well as for others who aspire to understand them), but it also reproduces that culture.

ASSESSING THE ARGUMENT

Given the goals of symbolic ethnographers, it is not surprising that their accounts are marked by certain features that Geertz has characterized as "methodological pitfalls to make a Freudian quake" (1973d:452). These pitfalls involve the difficulties of verifying an interpretation, of systematically assessing its claims (cf. 1973b:16, 24). However, in appraising interpretive ethnography, the reader may follow guidelines used in evaluating any kind of argument. That is, the reader can examine the kinds of claims an argument contains and the kinds of data it uses to support those claims. In Geertz's ethnography, there are three kinds of claims: those supported by data, those unsupported by data, and those that are unwarranted by the data provided.

Geertz supports his depiction of the cockfight primarily by reference to and explication of Balinese cultural categories and norms. He gives the native terms for the components of this event. The fight (sabungan), held in a ring (wantilan), is divided into several matches (sehet). Once a match is made, spurs (tadji) are attached to the animials (sabung), and they fight for brief periods (tjeng), during which their handlers (pengangkeb) are not allowed to touch them. The fight ends when one of the animals is killed. Geertz also describes the rules, preserved in manuscripts (lontar, rontal), which are supposed to govern the fighting, as well as the umpire (saja komong, djuru kembar) who enforces them.

He also describes the gambling that takes place at a cockfight, a most significant aspect of the event, since, as he claims, it links the fight to the "wider world of Balinese culture" (1973d:429). In this sense, Geertz sees gambling as the key to understanding the meaning of the cockfight and the culture from which it is drawn. As with other aspects of the event, Geertz presents verbal data to support his claims about cockfight wagering. He identifies two kinds of bets, a center bet (toh ketengah) and a side bet (toh kesai). He also indicates the language of betting and its general patterns. The two kinds of bets have different characteristics. The center bet is typically large, the sum being raised by and representing a social group, and is an even bet. The side bet, by contrast, is usually small, made by an individual, and given or taken with odds. It is the large center bet that makes a cockfight interesting to the Balinese, giving it its significance or, as Geertz describes it, its "depth" (1973d:431). Having described the wagering in these terms, Geertz then considers why a large center bet match is interesting to the Balinese, a question that leads him to an analysis of its meaning.

For Geertz, one meaning of wagering in the Balinese cockfight is sociological, and he interprets its significance by relating it to other features of Balinese social structure. Thus, he claims that the center bet is deep, and therefore meaningful, because it expresses social status and social relationships. It is not winning or losing money that is at issue—in the long run the amount exchanged balances out—although that is not to say that money is unimportant to the Balinese. Rather, the center bet pits the bettors, and the groups they represent, against one another, simulating the alliances and oppositions that occur in social life.

To document the relationship between the cockfight and social structure, Geertz describes several facts about Balinese villages and about bettors and the ways in which they bet. He does not actually present the data that supports these claims; rather, he assures the reader of their existence (cf. 1973d:437). Basically, the betting reflects a segmentary social system. Thus, men should back a cock owned by a member of their own kin group when opposed by one belonging to another kin group. Correspondingly, bettors support the animal of an allied group against one from an unallied group (that is, an animal from one's own village against one from another village, and so on). Geertz claims that betting on a cockfight does not create fission or fusion; rather it expresses village and kin group alliances, rivalries, and hostilities which are the result of still other social processes, and it does so in a way—in "play form" (1973d:440)—that does not lead to open conflict. Geertz emphasizes that point: fundamentally the cockfight dramatizes "status concerns" (1973d:437). Whatever its sociological function, the cockfight also expresses Balinese values and beliefs about men and about human nature. In conveying Balinese ethos and worldview, Geertz, like Evans-Pritchard before him, depends upon verbal evidence. In one example, Geertz argues that the cockfight symbolically expresses Balinese thinking about the "sociomoral hierarchy" of men: at one end of the scale is the revered, high-status man, the "true cockfighter" (*bebatoh*); at the other end is the disdained, low status "driven gambler" (*potet*) (1973d:435). In another, he supports his claim that the cockfight reveals Balinese values of order and disorder with reference to contrasting concepts: *rame* is a word that describes not only a cockfight, but also a noisy, crowded, and desired social state; *paling* is the term that describes not only the confused and disoriented whirling of the fighting roosters, but also a general state of social disarray (1973d:446). The evidence Geertz presents confirms his contention that the cockfight is a Balinese event and that it has a structure conceptualized by them.

However, Geertz also makes claims about the cockfight that are not supported by evidence. For example, he presents no data to support his assertions about its psychological function. He asserts that a "text" is a "symbolic form" which functions "in concrete situations to organize perceptions (meanings, emotions, concepts, attitudes)" (1973d:449). Yet no evidence presented warrants conclusions about how Balinese think or feel about themselves or their society. Whereas the language and rules of the cockfight are described in detail, perceptions are simply attributed to Balinese.

Moreover, although Geertz posits that the cockfight, for a Balinese, contributes to the "creation and maintenance" of an awareness of his personality and culture (1973d:451), he offers no measurements of cognitive states at any one point in time, let alone before and after exposure to or participation in a cockfight. This is an important omission because claims about creating and maintaining consciousness would require data about changes in mental or emotional states, data drawn from at least two points in time. Similarly, Geertz argues that in "the cockfight, the Balinese forms and discovers his temperament and his society's temper at the same time" (1973d:451). Yet, he presents no data that warrant claims about a state of mind or addresses the issues of how a state of mind has been formed or how people come to be informed about it.

In short, Geertz develops his interpretation of the interpretive function of the Balinese cockfight by stating and restating his claims without providing data that substantiates them. He presents no evidence for accepting his reading of the "text."

Several scholars have commented on the problem of assessing the credibility of claims in symbolic ethnographies (for example, Walters 1980, Roseberry 1982, Shankman 1984, Crapanzano 1986). For example, Geertz claims that when the owner of a winning cock takes the body of the losing cock home to eat, "he does so with a mixture of social embarrassment, moral satisfaction, aesthetic disgust, and cannibal joy" (1973d:421), to which Crapanzano remarks: "We must ask: on what grounds does he attribute 'social embarrassment,' 'moral satisfaction,' 'aesthetic disgust' (whatever that means) and 'cannibal joy' to the Balinese? to all Balinese men? to any Balinese man in particular?" (1986:72). Another example is Geertz's claim that Balinese attend cockfights to discover the character of men and the nature of social life (cf. 1973d:450). Not only does he not offer evidence for this interpretation of what motivates the Balinese, but he also asserts that they go to cockfights for quite different reasons—to raise funds, to gamble, to dramatize status (cf. 1973d: 414, 425, 437)—again without presenting the grounds on which such statements are based. The absence of data has led one observer to state that "Geertz offers no specifiable evidence for his attributions of intention, his assertions of subjectivity, his declarations of experience" (Crapanzano 1986:74) and another to assert that because Geertz "sometimes ignores basic . . . rules for the presentation of ethnographic evidence . . . thick description sometimes appears to come out of thin air" (Connor 1984:271).

There is also a problem of generalization. Geertz writes as though his interpretation applies to all Balinese (cf. 1973d:417, 419, 420, 425, 431, 433, 434, 440, 442, 445, 446, 447, 449, 450), although he also refers to a presumably typical Balinese man (1973d:420, 433, 435, 450, 451). He makes such claims, despite the fact he also asserts that there are different sorts of Balinese—people with different sorts of status and different sorts of experiences—who presumably attach different meanings to cockfights. Balinese women, for example, do not attend cockfights (1973d:417) and Balinese men of differing social status differentially participate in the cockfights and the betting that takes place at them, including "the true cockfighter" and the "driven gambler," for each of whom the cockfight has a different meaning (1973d:435–36). In short, Geertz implies that the cockfight as a symbolic event has the same meaning for all Balinese, an implication that is unwarranted by the evidence he presents.

Perhaps even more problematic for Geertz's interpretation of the cockfight is another type of generalization made in "Deep Play." Although the cockfight is presented as a window into the wider Balinese culture, it is, as Geertz acknowledges, only one event in which "Bali surfaces" (1973d:417). There are other events, other symbols, from which a reading of Balinese culture may be drawn, and, which, in so far as such events differ, would lead to different interpretations of it. As Geertz states (1973d:451–52),

> The ceremony consecrating a Brahmana priest . . . expresses tranquility not disquiet. The mass festivals at the village temples, which mobilize the whole local population in elaborate hostings of visiting gods . . . assert the spiritual unity of village mates against their status inequality and project a mood of amity and trust. The cockfight is not the master key to Balinese life, any more than bullfighting is to Spanish. What it says about that life is not unqualified nor even unchallenged by what other equally eloquent cultural statements say about it.

Thus, it is the ethnographer's choice of the symbolic event for analysis that colors the particular interpretation of the wider culture in which it occurs. And it works the other way as well. The ethnographer's vision of the culture shapes his or her selection of "text" to be read and the meanings he or she attributes to it.

ANOTHER EXAMPLE OF SYMBOLIC ETHNOGRAPHY: SHERPAS THROUGH THEIR RITUALS

Ortner's *Sherpas Through Their Rituals* (1978) also exemplifies symbolic analysis as a style of ethnography. Its aim is to understand the nature of Sherpa society through an analysis of the meanings of certain rituals in Sherpa culture. As such, it resembles Geertz's attempt to grasp the inner nature of Balinese society and the wider world of Balinese culture through an interpretation of the Balinese cockfight. It also resembles Evans-Pritchard's structural analysis in *The Nuer*: it identifies forces that undermine social order, it posits a solution to the problematic nature of societal cohesion, and it offers as evidence for its interpretation an analysis of a people's cultural categories and social norms.

Ortner is explicit about the analytical framework of her ethnography. Her goal is to "open" Sherpa culture to readers, "unfolding it, revealing it, providing not only a sense of surface form and rhythm, but also a sense of inner connections and interactions" (1978:1). She approaches this end by describing the ways in which the Sherpas understand themselves and their world, an understanding, Ortner asserts, that is expressed in Sherpa rituals. [She focuses on rituals because, she claims (cf. 1978:1), they are events that dramatize (as the Balinese cockfight dramatizes), for both participant and observer, the assumptions that underlie, organize, and make intelligible Sherpa social life.]

[This methodology is appropriate, she contends (cf. 1978:5), because rituals shape the understanding that people have of themselves and of their world.] Like Geertz before her, Ortner argues that in the actions, operations, and motions of ritual, the consciousness of participants is manipulated and the significance of their way of life is imparted to them. Ortner posits that this ritual process is necessitated by "the conflicts and contradictions of social experience and cultural meaning that are encoded in, and alluded to by, the ritual symbolism" (1978:3). Such problems undermine a people's orientation to and grasp of what is meaningful in their world, without which they are unable to live effectively and satisfactorily in it. [Thus, rituals provide answers to the problematic features of social life in the sense that they present an opportunity for people to examine (and reexamine) the basic presuppositions they hold about themselves and their world.] These cultural premises underlie the intelligibility of social life, shaping the Sherpas' attitudes and actions.

THE ARGUMENT OF THE ETHNOGRAPHY

Ortner develops her analysis of the meanings embodied in Sherpa rituals by specifying the problems of Sherpa life that are supposed to be addressed in them. [The basic problem of the Sherpas is the challenge to the stability and solidarity of communal life.] Sherpa values, and in particular the tenets of Buddhism observed by the Sherpas, underlie the potentially fissile character of Sherpa society. The religion, Ortner claims, fosters "tendencies toward isolation and atomization," which she concludes, threaten the "fabric of Sherpa society" (1978:162). These values, Ortner asserts, represent "forces of anarchy" (1978:90; cf. 137, 162). In this sense, Sherpa Buddhism is analytically analogous to Nuer interest in cattle: both shape a worldview that defines ends, the pursuit of which potentially undermines social relationships.

Also like the Nuer, the problem of societal cohesiveness among the

Sherpas is magnified by the lack of devices for conflict resolution. The Sherpas have "no formal mechanisms of social control" (1978:26), which, given their antirelational bias, further subverts the basis for communal stability. Thus, the depiction of Sherpa social structure as composed of nuclear families within which relationships are fragile and between which there are few and tenuous ties, in addition to the absence of institutionalized means for dealing with socially disruptive behavior, leads Ortner to question how Sherpa society is possible. As she puts it, ["What keeps things in order?"] (1978:26). For Ortner, as for Evans-Pritchard, the problem posited is that of the ways in which the potential for disorder is contained.

[Ortner answers her question in two parts. She first claims that "the Sherpas depend on internalized constraints" (1978:26) to prevent antisocial behavior. However, as Ortner observes, "inner constraints do not always constrain" (1978:26). Therefore, Ortner looks elsewhere for the basis of Sherpa social order and finds it in their rituals. She concludes then that rituals resolve conflict by offering "solutions" to the "problems" implied in the rituals, problems that exemplify particular instances of the potential for disorder.]

These solutions, according to Ortner, function psychologically. She argues that ritual enables its participants to think about themselves, and especially about their feelings and the forces that motivate them, in ways that foster adjustment to and acceptance of their way of being. In this sense, [rituals among the Sherpas serve the same function that cockfights do among the Balinese. They are models of and models for social reality. Ortner's interpretation follows Geertz's paradigm: [rituals manipulate and shape consciousness, they create meaning, and they restructure perceptions, feelings, and interpretations (cf. 1978:5, 6).]

TEXTUAL ORGANIZATION

[Ortner's interpretation of Sherpa life and of the meanings of their rituals is reflected in the organization of the ethnography. She uses the first chapter to introduce the reader to the theory and methods of symbolic anthropology. In the second chapter, she states the analytical problem of her study (that is, the problematic nature of Sherpa society) and outlines the nature of her conclusions (that is, rituals provide a means for resolving the conflicts and contradictions of Sherpa life and thereby contribute to social solidarity and stability). The next four chapters, which Ortner describes as the core of her symbolic analysis (cf. 1978:32, 127), are devoted to detailed analyses of the meaning of Sherpas rituals. In the last chapter, she reiterates her conclusions and draws out their implications for broader theoretical issues.]

The thrust of Ortner's interpretation is illuminated by an examination of the steps of her argument. This is evident in the sequencing of the chapters themselves, especially those describing and analyzing Sherpa rituals (chapters 3–6). Thus, Ortner begins her account with an analysis of a ritual that addresses strains within the Sherpa family. Ideally, Ortner claims, the Sherpa family is autonomous and self-sufficient, a "closed" unit, differentiated from and "opposed to the rest of society" (1978:39). Within the family relations should be solidary, characterized by warmth and "relaxed intimacy" (1978:39). The family, in Sherpa thought, is "a sort of 'refuge' from the world 'outside'" (1978:39). In short, Ortner concludes, the Sherpa family is ideally "tight" and "introverted," its members economically independent of other families but dependent on one another, and strongly tied to one another emotionally, especially children and mothers.

In contrast to these ideals, Ortner asserts that in reality relations within the Sherpa family are undermined by several factors. For one, children grow up and get married, forming their own families and leaving emotionally, and usually physically, the ones in which they were raised. Moreover, the formation of these new families creates economic strains for the old ones: the costs of a marriage, the disruption of the family as a work force, and the division of family property. Furthermore, as children mature and parents age, there are other difficulties: conflict between mother-in-law and daughter-in-law (especially when a son remains in the household of his childhood), the stresses of role reversal when children become the caretakers of their elderly parents, and the sense of loss and betrayal experienced by parents as children take their places and their resources.

This discrepancy between ideal and actual creates a tension that is supposed to be relieved in a ritual of atonement. This ritual addresses problems manifest in the developmental cycle; it is, however, especially meaningful for the elderly and serves to help them put their experience of disengagement in a positive light. It is supposed to help the elderly see themselves not as deprived but as approaching the cultural (that is, religious) ideal of autonomy. Cognitively and emotionally, loss is transformed into gain.

Not only are there tendencies toward conflict and instability within the family, but the same forces of "atomism" potentially disrupt relationships between families. Ortner argues that this threat is overcome by Sherpa beliefs about "hospitality," a way of "being social" that is normatively governed by rules of "etiquette" (1978:62). This is the subject of the next step in Ortner's argument.

Consistent with the autonomy and independence of their families, Ortner claims that Sherpas are reluctant to engage in the exchange of material goods, wary of the attachments that it may generate. This attitude potentially undermines social relationships, a situation that is supposedly addressed and overcome in the Sherpa customs of *yangzdi* (1978:63, 68, 90) and "hospitality" (1978:78). *Yangzdi* is an institutionalized transaction consisting of a gift of food (or beer), which obligates its recipient to reciprocate with a favor of some sort. The norms of hospitality, most evident at parties, govern host/guest relationships, including pressures to enact these roles. Having described in detail Sherpa beliefs about giving and receiving and the situations in which social exchanges take place, Ortner concludes that *yangdzi* "is the basic mechanism for generating exchange in Sherpa society" and that hospitality "dramatizes order ... produces order ... and reproduces a mechanism—yangdzi—for generating order ..." (1978:90).

In sum, in chapters 3 and 4 Ortner addresses antirelational tendencies within and between families. Within the family, the issue is how to resolve the threat to family relationships, and especially the feelings of loss experienced by the elderly, associated with the normal course of the developmental cycle of the domestic group. The answer, embodied in the ritual of atonement, is to encourage compassion and to define old age as approaching the cultural ideal of autonomy. Between families, the issue is how to resolve the threat to communal relations associated with the self-sufficiency and closed nature of families. The answer, embodied in the rituals of hospitality and institutionalized gift-giving, is to foster exchange and reciprocity between households.

But even with these efforts to overcome the tendency toward atomism, there are still obstacles to the maintenance of social order. As Ortner argues, the "forces of anarchy and disruption periodically return, in the form of demons, to wreak chaos and pollution in society" (1978:90). Therefore, she turns to an examination of the ritual mechanisms by which demons are controlled. She does this in the next two chapters (chapters 5 and 6). The first of these two describes rituals of exorcism, in which Sherpas directly confront, by symbolic means, the disruptive forces represented by demons, and the second describes rituals of oblation, in which Sherpas attempt, through acts of giving similar to those of hospitality observed among the Sherpas themselves, to persuade their gods to assist them in combatting the demons that plague them.

In each of these chapters, Ortner claims that the function of these rituals is to transform the ways in which the Sherpas think and feel about themselves and others, thereby enabling them to overcome the forces that are potentially disruptive of their social order. This interpretation is reiterated throughout the ethnography, exemplified in such claims as: the ritual of atonement repositions the individual to interpret abandonment as autonomy (cf. 1978:52, 55, 59); the conventions of hospitality induce in individuals a positive attitude toward exchange (cf. 1978:81); an exorcism ritual helps the individual to overcome the anxiety produced by anticipation of physical deterioration and death (cf. 1978:127); and an offering ritual lends individuals insight into their emotions, thereby producing a constructive way of dealing with their feelings of anger (cf. 1978:140, 147, 151).

CLAIMS AND DATA

The argument of the monograph is neatly presented, its claims repeatedly stated and systematically interwoven. However, claims should be assessed in light of the evidence presented in support of them. Therefore, the reader must carefully examine the ethnographic data contained in the monograph, asking whether or not the evidence presented warrants accepting the ethnographer's interpretations.

When assessing the ethnographic evidence, it is important to identify the kinds of claims being made in the ethnography (its level of analysis), since they determine the kinds of data that will be relevant to its interpretations. *Sherpas Through Their Rituals* is a modes of thought analysis. This is clear from Ortner's remarks throughout the ethnography: she writes of the Sherpas' "point of view" (1978:35), of Sherpa "notions" (36, 38, 39, 70, 133, 136); of what is "ideal" (1978:39, 44, 45, 135); of what should happen "in theory" (1978:39, 44, 46, 73); of Sherpa "images" (1978:39); of Sherpa "thought" (1978:41, 67, 74, 113); of the "cultural view" (1978:43); of "folk interpretations" (1978:43, 133); of what Sherpas "see" and "say" (1978:49, 70, 79, 82, 98); of "cultural explanations" (1978:53, 58, 145); and of the statements of "informants" (1978:72, 73, 86, 133).

Consistent with this level of analysis, the evidence she presents for the ritual performances themselves consists primarily of what Sherpa say, including their concepts, proverbs, myths, and legends. For example, in analyzing the ritual of atonement, Ortner provides native terms for the ritual (*nyungne*), for various ceremonies that comprise it (for example, *sang, tso*), and for the deity (Pawa Cherenzi—in Tibetan, sPyan-ras-gzigs) to whom it is directed.

The ethnographic data for the other rituals are similar to those presented in the description of the ritual of atonement. For example, in analyzing the ways in which the ritual of hospitality informs Sherpa social life, Ortner describes the conduct expected at Sherpa parties (the salient context for hospitality), their categories for kinds of parties (for example, *gyowa*), and native terms for and proverbs about transactions that occur in them (*yangdzi*). The etiquette of hospitality, intended to overcome the reluctance of Sherpas to engage in solidarity-producing exchanges between members of different households, is backed by moral sanctions, evident in Sherpa concepts (for example, *pem*) and proverbs (for example, *kha tongba loksin, kha tong gasung*).

In describing rituals of exorcism and offering, the data are also cultural categories and social norms. Thus, Ortner indicates that there are Sherpa terms for protective rites in general (*kurim*) and for particular rites (for example, *do dzongup, gyepshi, kangsur*, and *tso*). She also describes in detail the normative rules of these rites, including terms for their artifacts, actors, and actions. For example, in exorcism rituals tiger figures (*sende*) are destroyed by soldiers (*peshangba*), and thread crosses (*do*) and an effigy of a ritual's sponsor (*lut*) trap or otherwise distract demons (*du* and *de*), who represent greed. In offering rituals, there is a purification rite (*sang*), and offerings (including *chepa, serkim, tso, chinche, nangche, sangche,* and *torma*) presented to the gods, who are symbolized by figures made of dough (also classified as *torma*). In these rituals, people ask the gods for help in combatting demons and other disruptive forces, including feelings of anger.

[Although Ortner includes Sherpa concepts in describing their rituals, she puts them to other uses as well. She refers to them in explicating the problematic features of Sherpa society and the solutions to be found in the rituals.] Thus, in explaining the reasons for observing the ritual of atonement, Ortner refers to Sherpa terms for seeking merit (*payin*), and its contrasting concept, demerit or sin (*dikpa*), as well as those for acts that are viewed as meritorious (*gyewa-zhinba*). She then relates these concepts to the antirelationalism of Sherpa culture: seeking merit in Sherpa (Buddhist) thought is related to striving for detachment from others, a tendency that leads to the isolation of families. Ortner therefore concludes that the Sherpa family is a closed unit, a hypothesis that she supports by including Sherpa proverbs that suggest that the family is a "refuge" from the strife and stresses of the "outside" world (1978:39, 173) and symbols of family/household boundedness, including Sherpa concepts (for example, *yang* or luck) and ceremonies (for example, *yang-guup* intended to regain or preserve the luck of the family). The ritual of atonement is supposed to be a corrective for antirelational attitudes. It does this, she claims, by fostering a sense of "compassion" (*nyingje*) in people, who are supposed to identify with the god Cherenzi, who is benign and peaceful (*shiwa*) rather than fierce and violent (*takbu*). In short, Ortner uses Sherpa cultural categories as evidence of both their rituals and the wider belief system in which they are located.

EVALUATING SHERPAS THROUGH THEIR RITUALS

As in other symbolic studies, Ortner's account of Sherpa rituals has its methodological pitfalls. She describes in detail the structure of Sherpa rituals, including the roles of their participants, the normative rules that govern them, and material objects used in them. The evidence consists not only of Sherpa concepts, normative statements, and proverbs, but also of seven photographs, including those of the ethnographer's cook and translator (and his wife and child) (1978:2), of men eating at a picnic (1978:62), of a wealthy woman and her daughter (1978:92), of a "reincarnate" lama (1978:129), of a figure of a deity (1978:34), and of views of the Sherpa environment and a Sherpa village (1978:11, 13). There are also eight line drawings, representing a model of a seating arrangement (1978:75), ritual artifacts (1978:94, 134), models of a ritual alter (1978:96, 146), and Ortner's classification of aspects of the Sherpa "self" (1978:104) and of her comparison of Tibetan and Sherpa actors and figurines (1978:116).

However, this account of ritual scenes and scenarios does not provide evidence for their alleged functions, "subjective" or "social" (1978:151). Claims about the shaping of consciousness, the creation of meaning, and the restructuring of perception are unsupported by evidence about how people think or feel. There are no data, for example, regarding the mental state or subjective orientation of any Sherpa, either before or after participation in, or exposure to, a ritual performance. Ortner presents no data about changes in attitudes or actions, evidence that would be necessary to document claims about transformations people are supposed to have experienced. Rather the claims are simply stated and restated, although Ortner alludes to the "processes," "devices," and "mechanisms" by which she thinks such changes are induced (cf. 1978:6, 8, 36, 48, 51, 54, 150–51).

Ortner recognizes the problems in documenting claims about consciousness. She acknowledges difficulties in verifying attributions of mental states, but nevertheless assumes that describing the structure of events reflects their participants' experiences of them (cf. 1978:5). This is a crucial point for Ortner's argument. She presents a warrant for her claims about what ritual does (that is, that ritual behavior shapes psychological states), even though she presents no data for such outcomes, and, moreover, will not do so, since she assumes that such outcomes, if they exist, are the result of the ritual process. This is circular reasoning. It also raises the question: for whom is there a restructuring of meaning? This is especially problematic, since she does not address the question of who, if anyone, in fact has such an experience.

If Ortner is concerned with how symbols shape the ways in which people see, feel, and think about the world and with ritual as "one of the primary matrices for the reproduction of consciousness" (1984:154), an important question is what constitutes appropriate evidence for claims about such processes. It is not sufficient to describe a ritual or other practice and use that description of what people do as evidence of what they see, feel, and think.

Ortner presents no data that such states of consciousness are achieved. In the case of the ritual of atonement, no data are given that substantiate Ortner's claims that Sherpas think, feel, or otherwise experience identification with the deity or the compassion that such a transformation would imply. Moreover, Ortner presents no data in support of her claims that "party etiquette reproduces certain subjective *conditions* for exchange"

(1978:81), that it "may be seen as a sort of rehearsal and shaping of con-sciousness for experiences of genuine (would-be) exchange" (1978:82), or that hospitality "dramatizes order . . . produces order . . . and reproduces a mechanism . . . for generating order beyond the party itself" (1978:90). Nor does she provide data, verbal or otherwise, that support her claims that in these rituals people experience relief from the demons who embody "forces of anarchy" or resolve and master disruptive feelings of anger.

What kinds of data would be relevant to such claims? For example, how could Ortner better make her case for the order-producing function of hospitality? One possibility is to examine the correlation between the occur-rence of this secular ritual and that of disorder. That is, the ethnographer could present to the reader evidence that in communities where acts of hos-pitality flourish (however measured) there disorder (however measured) is minimal, and, conversely, where there are few acts of hospitality, there disor-der reigns. Another possibility, even more to the point of creating meaning, would involve a comparison of types of consciousness and levels of order before and after exposure to or participation in hospitality events.

[This same line of reasoning can be applied to the overall argument. For example, if Sherpa society is atomistic and ritual creates and/or restores solidarity, then it would follow that where ritual, there solidarity, and, con-versely, where no ritual, there anarchy.] To assess this claim, the analyst would have to examine variation in social solidarity, across different situa-tions or communities. Is there evidence, or any indication of evidence, that could be used to this end? There appears to be. For example, Ortner indi-cates that sometimes Sherpas achieve solidarity and sometimes they do not (cf.1978:xi), implying the existence of contrasting situations necessary for a controlled comparison. Moreover, the village in which Ortner did most of her fieldwork and from which she draws most of her observations, was unusual, being larger and better off than other villages and dominated by a single clan (cf. 1978:14, 16, 19). Perhaps the size of the village is related to the presence of solidarity-inducing rituals, a hypothesis that could be tested by examining whether or not rituals are less frequently performed or have different meanings in smaller, and perhaps less solidary, villages or in those that are not dominated by a single clan. And, as in the case of hospitality, an appraisal of claims concerning changes in consciousness and the sociological consequences of them would require examining people's attitudes and actions before and after their participation in parties and other situations of exchange.

[Just as there are no data to support Ortner's interpretation of the psy-chological function of Sherpa rituals, there is little evidence to support her view of the problematic features of Sherpa society.] She claims that Sherpa society is atomistic, divided into isolated, antisocial nuclear families, themselves composed of individuals whose view of human nature is supposed to be that it is fundamentally penurious, avaricious, materialistic, and emphatically egocentric. Yet this view is not based on facts presented in Ortner's account. Indeed, Ortner acknowledges that others see the Sherpas quite differently, as does she. She remarks:

> Readers who have had contact with Sherpas, and who have found them to be warm, friendly, hospitable, and generous (as I did), will find it peculiar that I talk about anti-social tendencies in Sherpa society. . . . [These] discussions of the "closed family," of difficulties of exchange, and so forth, are *analytical* discussions. . . . Similarly, the discussion about demons and exorcisms may lead the reader to imagine that Sherpa religion is a religion of fear. . . . But the Sherpas do not walk around in a state of religious anxiety, and I wish here to correct any such impression that might be conveyed by my discussion. (1978:xi–xii; cf. 10).

Furthermore, she concedes that the Sherpas do have solidary communal relationships. Although the nuclear family may be the effective unit in daily life, it is part of a wider network of enduring relationships and mutual assistance (cf. 1978:22). Sherpas themselves conceptualize a wider group, described as "village people," between whom there are ties of support and other exchanges (1978:23). Ortner also alludes to evidence that undermines her view of the Sherpas as living in anarchy: she states that among them crime is infrequent and murder nonexistent (cf. 1978: 26–27). Finally, Ortner's account of Sherpa hospitality contradicts her representation of the atomized community. She writes that the "Sherpa village is a community, with lively social interaction, a reasonable degree of order and solidarity, and often a certain collective identity" (1978:61).

These claims (and they too are only claims—Ortner presents no evidence to confirm them) confound the overall argument in *Sherpas Through Their Rituals*, casting doubts on the proposition that social order is a problematic feature of Sherpa society. This issue resembles Evans-Pritchard's interpretation in *The Nuer* that a segmentary system creates and maintains social order in the face of conditions that threaten to undermine it, without presenting evidence that social order is in fact empirically problematic. That is, Ortner posits a problem in Sherpa society that may not exist and presents, in her interpretation of Sherpa rituals, a solution for them that is unsupported by the data.

Thus, it appears that Ortner's account of the Sherpas is based on a claim—that they exhibit antisocial tendencies that are contained by their rituals—that is not grounded empirically. She even admits that it is inconsistent with her own experiences and observations as well as those of others, including the Sherpas. Rather the claim is consistent with and serves to advance her argument that rituals shape individual consciousness. Her emphasis on the "analytical" nature of her description and interpretation is remarkable: positing a potential problem of disorder positions the analyst to describe a mechanism (rituals) that is interpreted as enabling people to cope with the postulated problem.

There is another deficiency in Ortner's argument, one comparable to Geertz's treatment of the cockfight as representative of the whole of Balinese culture. That is, she selects for examination a set of rituals that may correspond to one aspect of Sherpa culture, but which clearly do not reflect other aspects of it and, more importantly for her argument, do not necessarily reveal the culture as a whole or even its most salient themes. Thus, starting from another analytical entry point—a different set of rituals, it is possible to construct an alternative interpretation of Sherpa life. For example, Ortner notes that during her fieldwork the ritual of atonement drew only eight people, whereas weddings are crowded and lively occasions, are the events that Sherpas like best, and emphasize connections between families (cf. 1978:56). Thus, an analysis of weddings would lead to a different interpretation of Sherpa society than that based on examining the ritual of atonement.

The contrast between the interpretations of the family and of Sherpa social life, drawn from an analysis of a religious ritual and from a description of secular weddings, raises a critical question for the reader. Why not *Sherpas Through Their Weddings?* Ortner's assertion that she did not have the space to more fully consider weddings or that analyzing them would take her beyond her primary concern with religious rituals (cf. 1978: 56, 174, 175) does not suffice. That topic is beyond the scope of the monograph, only given the ethnographer's choice of portraying the Sherpas in a specific way. To focus on weddings, and the ethos and worldview they imply, would require an altogether different interpretation of Sherpa culture.

The disparity between the views of the Sherpas and those of the analyst present another problem in accepting Ortner's argument. Remember that Ortner argues that rituals are supposed to reveal how the Sherpas see themselves (cf. 1978:1). Yet she informs the reader that her views and those of the Sherpas differ. Contrasts between the ethnographer's interpretation and those of Sherpas occur throughout the account (cf. 1978:43, 49, 50, 53, 59, 123, 147, 152–53). For example, where Ortner sees the Sherpas as conflict ridden, they regard themselves as friendly (cf. 1978:10). Or where Ortner sees Sherpa parties as ridden with competition and full of tension, they describe them as "fun" (*hlermu*) (1978:81).

There are also indications of different views among the Sherpas themselves.] For example, Ortner writes of the differences between "lay" and "orthodox" understandings (1978:36, 38, 39, 42, 48, 52, 98, 99, 133, 153, 163, 168), between Sherpas at different points in the life cycle (1978:58–60), and between those of different social status (1978:101–103).

[The different views expressed by Ortner and various segments of Sherpa society pose a dilemma for the reader of the ethnography. That is, where there are conflicting interpretations, whose point of view should the reader accept and on what evidence should that decision be made?] Were the ethnographer simply systematizing the views of the natives, these questions would perhaps be moot. But where that is not the case and/or where the people hold various views, the reader (as well as the ethnographer) is put in the position of having to weigh different interpretations against the available evidence.

[Not only is there a question of different views of Sherpa culture and society, but there is the issue of a difference between Sherpa concepts, beliefs, and values, and Sherpa practices.] Throughout the ethnography, Ortner comments on the contrasts between the ideal and real in Sherpa life (cf. 1978:19, 39, 43, 44, 45, 46, 64, 65, 73, 112). For example, she remarks that although Sherpas say that people should be compassionate toward everyone, in fact "beyond such verbal expression (and even genuine feeling), acts of true empathy and compassion . . . are rare in Sherpa society" (1978:43). Furthermore, she asserts, "generosity is highly valued . . . but rarely practiced consistently" (1978:65). [This discrepancy between ideal and real, between thought and action, raises an analytical problem: should Sherpas be interpreted in terms of how they are supposed to behave or in terms of how they actually behave.]

[Ortner and other symbolic ethnographers (like Geertz) seem to adopt the position (like Evans-Pritchard's) that behavior tends to accord with values and that values make behavior intelligible.] She focuses on Sherpa culture, as expressed in their (religious) beliefs, not because people live up to their ideals, but rather because "much of life takes place" in relation to them (1978:33). Like other structural or symbolic anthropologists, Ortner's point is that behavior is to be seen and understood in relation to a system of thought. However, when there is a discrepancy between the ideal and the real, there is no particular reason why the reader should accept the argument that it is this set of beliefs, rather than another, not considered by the analyst, that provides the best interpretation of people's behavior, or even that behavior, perhaps itself determined by nonnormative factors, shapes ideas.

There is also the related problem of Ortner's generalizations about the Sherpas, despite the fact that she acknowledges significant differences among them. Not only does Ortner argue at the level of Sherpa modes of thought, she also refers to Sherpas in general. She writes that "the Sherpa people" are the subject of her book (1978:10). Her claims are presented as though they apply to *all* Sherpas (cf. 1978: 41, 49, 50, 67, 71, 100). These statements make it clear that Ortner constructs her interpretation at the level of the system of beliefs and values, ignoring the actions of particular individuals and the circumstances under which they do and do not comply with cultural ideals and normative rules.

Ortner's focus on the system, rather than on what individuals actually do, is similar to that found in both structural and symbolic studies. It reflects the distinction Ortner makes between "strain" theory and "interest" theory. Ortner argues (1984:151–52),

> If actors in interest theory are always actively striving for gains, actors in strain theory are seen as experiencing the complexities of their situations and attempting to solve problems posed by those situations. It follows from these points that the strain perspective places greater emphasis on the analysis of the system itself, the forces in play upon actors, as a way of understanding where actors, as we say, are coming from. In particular, a system is analyzed with the aim of revealing the sorts of binds it creates for actors, the sorts of burdens it places upon them, and so on. This analysis, in turn, provides much of the context for understanding actors' motives, and the kinds of projects they construct for dealing with their situations (see also Ortner 1975, 1978).

In the following two chapters, we turn to studies that focus on individuals and their actions, examples of what Ortner has characterized as "interest" theory and of what I classified earlier as a "modes of action" approach to ethnography.

Chapter 4

ORGANIZATIONAL ETHNOGRAPHY

⌈Structural and symbolic analyses focus on cultural concepts and normative rules and on patterns of ideal behavior. That perspective produces ethnographies that emphasize what people are supposed to do and that pay less attention to the complexities of what people actually do. The decision to concentrate on modes of thought, however, leads to certain analytical limitations, including a disregard of the implications of the divergence between ideal and actual behavior and of the role of the individual in choosing from among alternative courses of action.⌉

In response to studies such as *The Nuer*, fieldworkers developed ethnographic accounts that addressed these issues. Several studies explored ways of presenting ethnography that would achieve these ends. Although these innovative works differ from one another, they all represent an extension of the conventions of structural analysis. They also display, however, continuities with that style of ethnography. Using terminology developed by Firth (1951, 1954, 1955) to characterize the new approach to ethnography, this chapter examines "organizational" ethnography. Its purpose is to depict the shift in level of analysis and kind of interpretation that mark this response to the perceived limitations of structural ethnography. It focuses on the kinds of questions that characterize action-oriented ethnographies. However, attention is also paid to developments in textual organization associated with the changes that emerged in anthropological argumentation and ethnographic accounts.

THE ANALYTICAL FRAMEWORK OF ORGANIZATIONAL ETHNOGRAPHY

The "organizational" point of view has become central to ethnography that stresses the study of transactions and social processes. Whereas structural ethnography emphasized the normative rules to which, it was assumed, people more or less conformed, Firth argued the case for examining the role of individuals in decision making, including choosing between alternative principles of behavior, and the social consequences of those decisions. He presented this goal of ethnographic description and analysis in *Elements of Social Organization* (1951) and later elaborated on it in two papers, "Social Organization and Social Change" (1964b [1954]) and "Some Principles of Social Organization" (1964c [1955]). This perspective was partially utilized in Leach's *Political Systems of Highland Burma* (1954), a classic in the social anthropological literature, which, like *The Nuer*, represents an effort to change the ways in which ethnography is interpreted and presented. It was more fully developed in later ethnographies, including Barth's *Political Leadership among Swat Pathans* (1959).

Firth focused on the individual decision maker acting within a framework of rules, opportunities, and nonnormative constraints. Although he acknowledged the necessity of examining structural issues as a first step in anthropological analysis, he emphasized the need to examine the relationships between principles and practice, drawing explicit attention to the alternatives for action for individuals and to the process of their selecting between them. The concept of social organization refers not to "structural principles" (1964b:45), but to what people actually do.

An "organizational" perspective extends attention from the normative rules of society to individuals as they choose to comply with or depart from those rules. Firth formulates the issue in this way (1964b:46): "The working arrangements by which a society is kept in being . . . rest upon individual choice and decision. Here is our great problem as anthropologists—to translate the acts of individuals into the regularities of social process."

The difference between an organizational analysis and a structural analysis is clear. From the point of view of the former, it is insufficient to present an ethnographic account that consists of abstract normative principles, since the enactment of those rules, and the roles implied by them, is often problematic. People, Firth notes (1964b:47), may recognize and honor their "rights and duties" or they may not. The ethnographer must attend to

both belief and behavior, analyzing when, and in what circumstances, individuals act as they should as well as when they do not.

[Different factors can influence the choices that individuals make.]
These include, in Firth's terminology (1964b:49–50), the "magnitude of the
situation," and the "alternatives open for choice and decision." An example
of magnitude would be a lack of fit between the number of positions and persons seeking to fill them, as when there are more people seeking employment
than the number of jobs available for them. This discrepancy would require
adjustments in the recruitment and training of workers, in the behavior of
workers, both employed and unemployed, in the policies and planning associated with unemployment benefits and other forms of social security, and in
the ideas commonly held about the meaning of work and its loss.

[An example of alternatives for action is evident in anthropological studies of the relationship between mother's brother and sister's son. As Firth notes
(1964b:50), a society may have a rule that stipulates a particular pattern of
behavior between individuals who occupy these roles. In structural analyses,
this is often discussed as an ideal type or a general case, ignoring the actual distribution of uncles and nephews. "But," Firth asks (1964b:50), "if there is more
than one of either, of if the mother has no brother, what happens?" He answers
that a discrepancy in the "numerical equivalence between mother's brothers
and sister's sons may necessitate considerable adjustments." These adjustments
might involve a classificatory kinsman (for example, a mother's father's brother's son) assuming the rights and duties of the role, but he might have nephews
of his own (the sons of his true sister) who have a claim on him. This might
entail "a conflict of obligation" and efforts to avoid such demands or even failure to meet them. All of these possibilities and their implications for other
behavior are of central importance in an organizational analysis.

For Firth, analysis of social organization follows that of structure. He
argues that conducting a structural analysis should precede the posing of
organizational questions, but he is also concerned with principles evident in
behavior itself. These principles reflect interaction between behavior and
organizational factors. They are not normative; rather they are defined by
Firth as "organizational principles" (1964c:74).

Organizational principles reflect the adjustments individuals make
when faced with organizational problems. For example, the "principle of
moderation or expediency" (1964c:74) represents accommodation in social
action to an inconsistency between, or inapplicability of, normative rules.
Another example of an organizational principle is that of the "economy of
effort" (1964c:80). Firth describes this principle as reflecting a matter of the
allocation of limited resources. Thus, when one person makes claims about
himself or herself in order to engage in some course of action, it is often the
case, he suggests, that such claims are taken by others at face value, since

the cost of verifying them is perceived as greater than the cost that would be incurred by failure to do so (and greater than the benefits resulting from a gain in confidence that may follow from such verification). In Firth's words: "no effort is normally made to check upon such claims; it is more economical of effort to accept them at face value and fit the claimant into the scheme of social action accordingly" (1964c:81). Presumably, this principle could be stated in hypothetical terms such as the effort to verify other's claims varies with the perceived costs and benefits of such effort and with those attached to the possible outcome of interaction with the other.

⌠Organizational principles are significant because they identify, conceptualize, and analyze what people do.⌡ Firth makes them explicit, although other anthropologists use them implicitly. For example, in *The Nuer* there is the hypothesis that the probability of bloodwealth compensation varies with the ease of enforcement or sanction implementation. It is implied that there is an adjustment at the level of practice to an organizational problem: viable action takes place despite normative rules that would preclude such action. ⌠The importance of Firth's approach is that it marks a change of emphasis in the questions anthropologists ask and in the ethnographic accounts they provide. This approach is taken up and more fully developed in the "action" ethnographies that begin to appear at the end of the 1950s. Before turning to an examination of them, it is useful to first consider a monograph that marks a transition between structural and organizational ethnographies.⌡

A TRANSITIONAL STUDY: POLITICAL SYSTEMS OF HIGHLAND BURMA

Leach's *Political Systems of Highland Burma* (1954) draws upon the tradition of structural analysis seen in *The Nuer*, but it also introduces an organizational point of view. (Firth wrote the Foreword to *Political Systems* and Leach, in his Acknowledgments [1954:xvii], thanks him "for teaching me most of what I know about anthropology.") Both monographs are concerned with understanding behavior in terms of the cultural categories and normative rules held by the people they describe. Just as Evans-Pritchard bases his interpretation on an analysis of Nuer notions (beginning with a classification of local communities—their "socio-spatial categories"), Leach builds his argument around an analysis of Kachin concepts (their "structural categories"). He describes the rationale for the presentation of his argument (1954:xii–xiii):

> Nearly one-third of this book consists of Chapter V entitled 'The Structural Categories of Kachin *Gumsa* Society.' It is concerned with

the interpretation of a series of verbal concepts and their interconnec-
tions. ... The argument is ... that the set of verbal categories ... form a
persistent structured set and that it is always in terms of such categories
as these that Kachins seek to interpret (to themselves and to others)
the empirical social phenomena which they observe around them.

Leach's analysis, however, differs from that of Evans-Pritchard in the
attention it gives to alternative courses of action available to people and the
conditions under which they are likely to choose from among them. Evans-
Pritchard states that "values are embodied in words," noting that "one cannot
understand their range of reference without considerable knowledge of the
people's language and of the way they use it, for meanings vary according to
the social situation. ... " (1940a:114). He does not, however, concentrate his
analysis on the variation implicit in such situational selection of significance.
He does not, that is, focus on the choices that individuals may make in interpreting one another's claims. Analyzing this sort of conceptual "ambiguity"
(1954:76, 106) is at the heart of Leach's study. As he writes (1954:xiii): "The
special interest of the Kachin material is that Kachin verbal usage allows the
speaker to structure his categories in more than one way." The central aim of
his monograph is to analyze the variable meanings Kachin attribute to concepts. With that shift in perspective, Leach extends ethnography from
accounts of the normative basis of the system—what people should do—to
analyses of the possibilities of behavior—what they could do.

[The significance of this change is evident in the ways in which the
ethnographers deal with the issue of the "plasticity" and "flexibility" of
social concepts](cf. Evans-Pritchard 1940a:220, Leach 1954:106, 148). For
example, while Evans-Pritchard briefly considers the ways in which normative rules are modified to accommodate changing sociodemographic and
political circumstances, Leach focuses on the role of that process in the
organization of social life. Thus, in The Nuer we are told that they and their
neighbors, the Dinka, live interspersed among each other (cf. 1940a:221-
24), and we also learn that cultural rules are stretched when Dinka are
incorporated into Nuer lineages by "becoming Nuer" (caa Nath) or by
"becoming a member of the community" (caa dil e cieng or caa ran wec)
(1940a:218, 221–22). Similarly, in Political Systems the reader is informed
that the Kachins and the Shans, the people among whom Leach worked, are
"almost everywhere close neighbors and in the ordinary affairs of life they
are very much mixed up together" (1954:2). Leach also describes a strategy
of manipulating "cultural identities" (1954:40) when Kachins become Shans
(sam tai sai) and when one sort of Kachin (gumsa) becomes another (gumlao)
(1954:9, 30, 47, 49, 222, 293–97). [Whereas this procedure is incidental to
Evans-Pritchard's analysis—it is viewed as a mechanism for maintaining

structural stability, it assumes crucial importance in Leach's concern with the dynamics of cultural change.]

Leach contends that the process by which individuals change their cultural identities, that is, change who they claim to be, is to be understood by examining the meanings people attribute to structural categories. He asserts (1954:104):["If then we are to understand the nature of Kachin social structure, we must examine the practical meaning of those verbal expressions which a Kachin uses when making statements about the subject matter which I, as anthropologist, call social structure."]

Leach's concern with the "practical meaning" of concepts and its relation to structural analysis is exemplified in his account of Kachin marriage rules. At the local level of Kachin society, a community consists of small patrilineages (groups of individuals connected through the male line) that are related to one another by marriage. Thus, marriage rules—who should or should not marry whom—provide the primary structural principles of community organization. These principles, Leach notes, are "implied" by, or, as Evans-Pritchard would write, "embodied in," the terms *mayu-dama* (1954:73–74). From the point of view of any individual in a Kachin community, every patrilineage within it may be described as belonging to one of three categories in terms of marriage rules: one's own lineage or one related closely enough to it to be subject to a ban on marriage (*kahpu-kanau ni*); wife-giving lineages (that is, lineages from which males of one's own lineage have recently taken wives) (*mayu ni*); and wife-receiving lineages (that is, lineages into which females of one's one lineage have recently married) (*dama ni*).

The Kachins have a "formal" rule about marriage that involves these categories. It is that a man may not marry into his own lineage or that of his *dama*, and a woman may not marry into her own lineage or that of her *mayu*. It is preferred for a man to marry into his *mayu* and for a woman to marry into her *dama*. Once a *mayu-dama* relationship is established between two lineages, it "must be perpetuated by further marriages" (1954:74, 76, 136). Leach contends that although this rule appears to be rigid and unworkable because it closely restricts the choice of mates, in practice the system works because the rule is circumvented. As he states (1954:76), the ability to circumvent rules "makes it possible for Kachins to talk *as if* they were conforming to *mayu-dama* regulations while in fact they are doing something quite different."

Leach develops his analysis of the ways Kachins get around their marriage rules by examining the meanings of Kachin terms. He begins with what Kachins mean when they speak of "marriage." Kachins have a word, *num* ("woman"), which may mean either legal wife or concubine. Legality turns on whether or not the woman has gone through a ceremony (*num shalai*) involving the transfer of bridewealth from the lineage of the male to that of the female. This payment legitimizes the woman's offspring, who are incorporated into the lineage of the man who makes the payment. In other words, the payment secures rights over the children; it is a payment for the service of the woman as a mother. Kachins may live together as man and wife, like a married couple, whether or not the *num shalai* ceremony is performed, but they are considered married only when it takes place. Thus, an analysis of the meaning of the concept of marriage reveals that relationships can be established to which the marriage rule does not apply. In this way, practice may be said to conform to, or at least to not contradict, normative rules.

This circumvention of the marriage rule is facilitated by other Kachin concepts. For example, a child born to a woman who has not undergone the *num shalai* ceremony is considered illegitimate (*n-gyi*), but can be legitimized, that is, can be made a member of a lineage, by a payment (*sumrai hka*), which incorporates it into the kin group of the man making the payment. This payment legitimizes children one at a time, in contrast to the *num shalai* payment, which provides legitimate status for children collectively, either before or after they are born. Thus, the concept of *sumrai hka*, in terms of which a father can legitimize one of his offspring without marrying the mother, enables a man to live with a woman who is the mother of his legal children, but to whom he is not formally married. Being unmarried, the lineage of the woman is not *mayu* to the lineage of the man, and, conversely, his is not *dama* to hers. Because the marriage rule is inapplicable to such relationships, it is not broken by them.

Another tactic for rule-bending by conceptual manipulation involves the Kachin notions of "ritual wealth objects" (*hpaga*) and of "substitution" (*sang ai*). Leach argues that Kachin relationships are expressed as debts (*hka*) which can be discharged or paid-off by ritual wealth objects (1954:144–48). For example, the payment required in a marriage ceremony includes a cow buffalo. When the man cannot provide a buffalo as required, it is possible, in Kachin practice, to substitute for it another item, such as a pig, which "represents" the buffalo.

Similarly, in Kachin theory, the amount of the bride wealth is set according to the status of the bride (1954:149–54). If this theory were observed, Leach contends, the system would probably break down, since the lineage of wife-givers is usually superior to that of wife-receivers, and the prospective husband would be unable to afford the requisite payment. Therefore, in practice, the amount of bridewealth can be adjusted to the status of the groom. This is possible because marriage payments are fixed as so many ritual wealth objects and the Kachin concept of substitution permits the value of such objects to vary with the social status of those who are party to the relationship. These concepts allow practice to be consistent with theory.

Just as structural categories such as *num shalai, sumrai hka, hpaga,* and *sang ai* permit normative principles to remain intact despite a lack of behavioral conformity to them, it is also possible to get around the rule by means other than sheer conceptual manipulation. Leach describes three other ways. One is when a Kachin marries into a lineage that is classified as neither *mayu* nor *dama*, as in the case of distantly related groups (*lawu-lahta*). This practice provides only limited opportunities to avoid the constraints of marriage rules, since once the marriage takes place, the link between the groups is changed to *mayu* or *dama*, and the marriage rule becomes relevant on future occasions.

Another way is when the rule is observed through a token marriage. The marriage rule states that once a *mayu-dama* relationship is established, it should be reinforced by other marriages between the lineages. Leach points out that it is possible to comply with this expectation with only a single recurrence in each generation. That is, as long as one couple from the paired lineages is married in each generation, the alliance between them is confirmed and the remaining lineage members are free to marry elsewhere.

The third way in which practice may deviate from principle does not rely on simple manipulation of the rule, but relates noncompliance with nonenforcement of sanctions. This interpretation recalls Evans-Pritchard's assessment that, regardless of the structural model of Nuer segmentation and social order, political cohesion varies with the size of the local group. The Kachin rules forbid a man to marry a woman from his own lineage or from a wife-receiving lineage. In fact, Leach notes, the "formal rules . . . are frequently broken" (1954:138); relationships that in theory are incestuous do occur. They are broken when the persons involved come from lineages that are not located in the same local community. Since their groups are not in close contact with one another, they are not forced to act in terms of the "incompatible obligations" that result when a person is simultaneously *mayu* and *dama* to the same local lineage. In this case, there is inconsistency between ideal and actual patterns of behavior because the Kachins, like the Nuer, may disregard their own rules when the consequences of doing so are negligible, as when sanctions are not easily enforced. (This is another example of the organizational principle of expediency.)

Given Leach's emphasis on the possibilities of action, how does it compare with earlier structural analyses? It is similar in that it constructs a model based on native ideas. It is different in that he focuses on the looseness of fit between principle and practice and on its implications for the operation of society. Yet he makes this argument without presenting data on behavioral regularities. Although he refers to "practice" and contrasts it with "theory" or "principle" (for example, 1954:76, 122, 148-49, 154, 159, 162–63, 167, 189, 194), he includes little or no data about the frequencies or distributions of any actual behavior, either of conformity to or deviance from an ideal rule. That is, his claims about what Kachins "usually" do, are "likely" to do, or "normally" do (for example, 1954:116–17), as well as other "generalizations" (1954:135) he makes about what Evans-Pritchard referred to as "actualities," are unsupported by behavioral evidence. In this respect, his argument takes place largely on the same level of analysis as that found in *The Nuer*. In short, it elaborates upon Evans-Pritchard's type of ethnography but does not radically depart from it.

THE POSSIBILITIES OF ACTION: POLITICAL LEADERSHIP AMONG SWAT PATHANS

Fredrik Barth's *Political Leadership among Swat Pathans* (1959) exemplifies an organizational point of view that marks a significant shift in constructing ethnographic accounts. Like earlier structural ethnographies, it is concerned with the role of values and normative principles in shaping social life. Its focus, however, is on the possibilities of action—the behavioral alternatives available to individuals—and the bases for choosing among them, embodying the perspective suggested in Firth's program for studying the processes of decision making and of viable action. In particular, Barth examines opportunities and the constraints that channel individuals' responses to them.

I begin this discussion of Barth's monograph by reviewing the questions it takes as problematic and the solution it provides. I then discuss the way in which its textual organization contributes to the interpretation it presents. Next, I examine the kinds of claims it contains and the kinds of data Barth uses to support his interpretations. Coincidental with emphasizing the analysis of action, Barth's monograph is also characterized by innovations in the types of data it utilizes and the uses to which they are put. Moreover, since the nature of one ethnographic style may be seen more clearly when contrasted with another, I compare, on several points, Barth's study with that of Evans-Pritchard, a comparison which Barth himself suggests (1959:105, 134).

ETHNOGRAPHIC PROBLEM AND SOLUTION

Political Leadership among Swat Pathans deals with the question of political organization in a society that is "acephalous" and "anarchic" (1959:12). It concerns the principles of political organization among some 400,000 people in a "land of freedom and rebellion" (1959:133). Although the socioeconomic and cultural contexts of the Pathans of the Swat valley in northwest Pakistan differ from those of the Nuer, the analytical problem of the study is similar to that explored in *The Nuer*. Both monographs concern the ways in which order is achieved and maintained among a bellicose people who, in the absence of an effective central government, use, or threaten to use, physical force to acquire culturally valued ends and to protect themselves against the acquisitiveness and aggressiveness of others.

For Swat Pathans, land is their basic interest and self-help is their primary defense against threats to holding it and to the wealth that derives from it. A landowner has to be prepared to fight to protect his land, which he does by "rallying supporters and followers" (1959:12). The landless, who are poor and powerless, seek security from a patron (who is typically a landowner, but who may also be a politically influential "holy man" or "saint") against hunger and the exploitation of others. Thus, patron and dependent become leader and follower. Yet, as Barth notes, the relationship is not stable: followers will abandon a leader who fails to provide for and/or protect them, turning to another who is, or is perceived by them, as more powerful (cf. 1959:73). Similarly, a landowner will also seek assistance, in political conflicts, from other landowners who are allies (cf. 1959:106). Thus, the organization of political life among Swat Pathans revolves around creating and maintaining relationships that are drawn upon in the struggle for protection and security of property and person. Accordingly, Barth analyzes the processes of mobilizing support within and between "politically corporate groups" (1959:72, 123).

A similar situation prevails among the Nuer. There, too, men seek protection against aggression through self-help. Evans-Pritchard states: "The club and the spear are the sanctions of rights" (1940a:169) and "It is the knowledge that a Nuer is brave and will stand up against aggression and enforce his rights by club and spear that ensures respect for person and property" (1940a:171). He adds, moreover, that a man draws on others for support in fights and that kin and neighbors become allies (1940a:158, 169).

However, the analyses of the processes through which followers and allies are mobilized differ between the ethnographers of the Nuer and Swat Pathans. Evans-Pritchard sees Nuer social order as the product of a segmentary system that supposedly integrates the whole society. The alignment of people in segments and the combination of such segments is determined, in theory, by a set of normative principles. Moreover, the Nuer segmentary system constitutes an equilibrium, a state that results from compliance with structural rules. Barth, on the other hand, sees order among Swat Pathans, who also have a segmentary system, as deriving from normative constraints along with the unintended consequences, the "unsought product," of individuals combining together in small groups "that meet in interaction and opposition" (1959:1) The "balance" or equilibrium in their system is the result of a continuing "realignment in alliance blocs," a process that is determined by changing opportunities and constraints that influence the strate-gies of leaders in giving and receiving political support.

In Barth's account, it is the choices of individuals in combining together that are critical in shaping Swat Pathan political organization. These are not simply determined by any set of structural rules. Accordingly, he builds his argument around an analysis of Pathan decision making and the logic that underlies it. Whereas Evans-Pritchard examines normative rules that are supposed to govern conduct between territorial units (for example, tribes and their subdivisions), Barth looks at "political action," which he defines as the "art" of creating "effective and viable bodies of sup-porters" (1959:4). Evans-Pritchard focuses on modes of thought, Barth on modes of action.

Barth's focus on the processes shaping the choices that individuals make contrasts with that in *The Nuer*. Individual Nuer face decisions in try-ing to achieve their goals or in managing conflicts with fellow members of local groups, but Evans-Pritchard does not take them as problematic. They also change their local group membership, but he does not analyze the impli-cations of such changes for the functioning of the political system. For Barth examining actions such as decision making and the making and breaking of alliances are a primary theoretical task in the study of Swat Pathan political organization. He argues that Swat Pathans achieve order as the outcome of interaction between small local groups, so analyzing these groups and their relationships are for him, as they are for Evans-Pritchard, essential to its study. His argument, however, focuses on how these groups are formed, how their membership is mobilized in the event of confrontations and conflicts, and how they relate to one another in the wider political system.

Among Swat Pathans, followers choose whether or not to join politi-cally corporate groups, the groups that they will join, those they will leave, and those in which they will remain. Similarly, leaders choose to form, maintain, or terminate alliances with other leaders. To understand these choices, Barth analyzes the relationships between the leaders of these groups and their followers and between leaders. His procedure is to focus on the leaders and the ways in which they try to attract and keep followers and to manipulate allies; hence, the title of the monograph.

Barth's focus on choice leads him to adopt certain methodological innovations. He emphasizes the study of "observable activities" (1959:2). His rationale is that the analysis of such activities, in conjunction with that of behavioral alternatives, possibilities, and constraints, permits inference of the "bases of choice." This procedure results in his using descriptions of events and actions, presented in the form of "cases," "examples," and "illus-trations," as evidence for his analysis.

The differential emphasis on choice in the two monographs is evident in the treatment of local groups, the basic unit in the political systems of both Nuer and Swat Pathans. Evans-Pritchard focuses on the relationships among local groups, disregarding their internal political processes. Indeed, he asserts that, "A village is a political unit in a structural sense, but it has no political organization" (1940a:180). Barth, on the other hand, stresses the internal organization of local groups as well as the relationships between them. His "central problem" is "to explore the kinds of relationship that are established between persons in Swat, the way in which these may be systematically manipulated to build up positions of authority, and the variety of politically corporate groups which result" (1959:2). *The Nuer* has chapters on different systems of relationships between groups (for example, political, lineage, and age-set), and *Political Leadership* has chapters on leaders, followers, and allies.

TEXTUAL ORGANIZATION

Barth's emphasis on matters of choice and decision making is evident in the textual organization of his argument, which he outlines and explains in the beginning of his ethnographic presentation. In short, he first formulates the problem of the monograph and presents the rationale for its argument (in chapters 1 and 2). Barth then proceeds (in chapter 3) to a discussion of the influence of structural principles on action. Next he examines neighborhood, marriage, and affinal ties as sources of choice in forming relationships. Where one lives and to whom one is married or related as an in-law are not permanent or irrevocable decisions and are subject to change. Although these relationships influence political choices, they are not, however, in themselves political. Barth thus continues his argument by analyzing the bases of political relationships. He examines (in chapters 5 and 6) how nonpolitical relationships are transformed into political ties within local communities. Then he describes (in chapters 7 and 8) how these relationships are mobilized by individual leaders to form politically active local corporate groups. Finally (in chapters 9 and 10), he analyzes relationships among political leaders and the groups they command; these alliances constitute a societywide political system. The whole argument is divided into two parts, with the first part of the book (chapters 1–6) depicting the internal organization of local political groups and the second part (chapters 7-10), the way in which these constitute intergroup alliances.

CLAIMS AND DATA

The interpretation of Swat Pathan political organization incorporates several levels of analysis. The argument interweaves discussion of modes of thought with that of the opportunities and constraints facing individuals in the pursuit of their goals and the strategic considerations underlying their selection of one or another course of action. Moreover, Barth uses different types of data relevant to different levels of analysis and to the different sorts of claims and interpretations he makes.

From a structural perspective, Barth analyzes the ideas in terms of which Pathans make the decisions that constitute their political organization. His evidence for the way Swat Pathans think consists of their concepts and normative rules. He examines, for example, their ideas about castes, descent groups, and local ritual associations. Thus, he notes that Pathans see themselves as divided into social strata, or "castes" (*quom*) which are hereditary, ranked occupational groups: membership in these groups constitutes one sort of constraint on the formation of social relationships. He also notes that landowners (*Pakhtuns*) are divided into partilineal descent groups (*khel*) and describes their characteristics and the norms governing conduct of their members. Ritual associations (*teltole*) are concerned with the life-cycle rites of birth, marriage, and death. He describes the rights and duties of membership in these groups, including those of attending ceremonies and providing and receiving help at them.

Similarly, Barth analyzes Pathan concepts about the nature of relationships that render nonpolitical ties potentially political. Pathans view any superordinate-subordinate relationship between people in one context as implying the same sort of link between them in others. For example, landowners and tenants are regarded as master and servant, as are employer and employee. Providing service of any kind, even in a restricted context or in exchange for pay, connotes to Pathans a general subordinate status. They do not conceptualize limited authority, but rather see superordinate status as a characteristic of the person. This generalization of leader/follower roles has direct implications for Swat politics, since a superordinate in any one context can use his authority in a political one.

In analyzing other relationships that have potential for political mobilization, Barth notes that most of them are not prescribed by formal rules of leadership or partnership. These relationships are found in economic, tenancy, recreational, and religious groups. Unlike territorial, caste, descent, and life-cycle ritual groups, these are formed around ties between leaders and followers. That is, each group consists of a leader and his several followers, each of whom has a "contract" with the leader but no formal relationships with other followers. Since people decide on which groups to join, their composition is variable, depending on context and is not determined by normative principles.

Barth sees leader-follower relationships as requiring constant maintenance and recurrent enactment. Both leaders and followers enter the relationship pursuing their self-interests. A leader provides goods and services in exchange for a follower's support in political conflicts. The leader must therefore continuously seek means to replenish and increase the resources he uses to attract and retain followers. On the other hand, followers continuously evaluate the benefits they receive from a leader as well as the costs of subordinating themselves to any one individual. Because resources and alternatives are subject to change, the tie between a leader and a follower is potentially unstable, as each assesses the degree to which his self-interest is enhanced.

Barth devotes particular attention to the cultural criteria in terms of which Pathans evaluate men who are leaders or who aspire to leadership. For example, he examines the standards in terms of which "chiefs" (*khan, nawab, malak*) are judged. Although a follower looks at the land and wealth of a chief when deciding to whom he will commit himself politically, material resources are not the only basis on which such a decision is made. He also estimates the likelihood that a chief will protect him and his interests against the aggression of others. In making that judgment, he relies on the chief's reputation or prestige, understood as a reflection of past actions as well as an indication of future behavior. A chief attracts followers by building and maintaining a reputation for defending his interests and, by implication, those of his followers. Such a reputation is critical because it is the basis on which "claims and counterclaims" are weighed in Pathan politics. A chief's reputation is a social index of his capacity and his resolve to carry out his threats and make good his claims. It represents an evaluation, by his followers as well as by his opponents, of his character and potential reactions, in terms of culturally defined standards. Barth analyzes reputation, then, in terms of Pathan ideas regarding the appropriate conduct of chiefs.

Two concepts, "honor" (*izat*) and "shame" (*sharm*) define the end points of a continuum in terms of which Pathans evaluate a leader's reputation. To gain respect, a chief is ideally expected to be "virile and impetuous, given to extremes rather than compromise, sometimes unwise, but always brave" (1959:81). These qualities are supposed to come into play whenever the chief's interests are threatened by encroachment, either upon his land or on the person and reputation of a wife or sister. Thus, "any insult, any action or condition which 'shames' a Pathan, requires him to defend his honor, if he is not to suffer permanent loss of respect and status" (1959:82). A man who owns land and wealth, but who lacks honor is not a strong contender for leadership.

A chief's reputation is particularly tested in situations in which he is expected to seek revenge in defense of his honor. The Pathan idea of revenge is an action equal to or greater than the original insult. That is, Pathan leaders are expected, in order to maintain their honor and thus their reputation, to engage in a game of escalating retaliation. They have to outdo the other in order not to lose ground. For a chief the "main method of defending honor" is by "blood revenge" (*badel*) (1959:83). Conflict that involves blood revenge constitutes a "feud" (*pokhto*). A leader who extracts revenge on those who have shamed or insulted him defends his honor and thereby commands the respect of his followers. For followers, such revenge is a demonstration of the leader's ability and resolve to defend his and their interests, thus warranting their loyalty and support.

Barth also discusses the concepts and standards in terms of which Pathans evaluate "saints" (*pir, baba, pacha, sahib*, among other native categories) who constitute another type of leader. Whereas the reputation of a chief depends on his acting in accord with Pathan concepts of honor, a saint is judged by the criteria of "holiness" and "piety" (1959:99), standards that contrast with those applied to a chief.

Barth also discusses Pathan ideas about land tenure, since it is in the context of competition for the control of land that individuals are mobilized politically. Each member of the land-owning caste (Pakhtun) has a "share" (*brakha*) of the land controlled by his lineage. The unit of land held by a lineage is its estate (*daftar*) and traditionally there was a system (*wesh*) by which land was realloted periodically among different segments of Pakhtun lineages in order to achieve an equitable distribution of land and its output. There is also land (*siri*) that is exempt from reallotment. Pakhtuns may give it to support a mosque, to a saint or mediator, to those who provide services to them, or to another chief. Such land is withdrawn from the inherited estate. The importance of such privately owned land is that it constitutes one mechanism for change in land ownership. Change in land ownership is also possible through the sale of an inherited share from one Pakhtun to another, in which case the seller loses his membership in the Pakhtun caste. In either case, it is possible for individual Pakhtuns to change their status in the land tenure systems and thus in the political system.

Barth's analysis of Pathan ideas is also evident in his discussion of their concept of an "assembly" (*jirga*) of landowners. This is a meeting restricted to Pakhtuns, where only those holding inherited land may speak. This right is significant since the assembly serves as a forum for the debates that constitute an integral aspect of political life. Since those entitled to participate are landowners who act as patrons for their followers and tenants, the assembly provides a hearing for the claims and counterclaims of followers as well as leaders. Moreover, there are social norms that govern conduct of its members which stipulate who may speak, in what fashion, and about what matters. Taken together, the assembly and its rules comprise the political arena of landowners. This arena and the other relationships (territorial, caste, descent, ritual, and leader-follower) represent the background of the options in terms of which the possible strategies of political action are interpreted.

[Although Barth's account of the actors in the political system and the bases of their authority is presented primarily at the level of a structural analysis, his delineation of the opportunities and constraints in Pathan political action goes beyond that implied in native concepts or norms. It reflects the analyst's interpretation of how the system works. He describes what, from his point of view, is "theoretically" possible and the constraints that make one or another alternative more or less feasible (1959:68).] For example, he sees two potential strategies open to landowners for manipulating the political system in their favor. They can either combine with one another to jointly exploit nonlandowners by appropriating a maximum share of the latter's income, or they can compete with one another over control of land, each attempting to increase his own profits at the expense of other landowners. Analyzing the ecological, economic, and demographic constraints on their actions, Barth demonstrates why landowners have no choice but to become leaders of landless men.

Barth's model of Swat Pathan political organization includes the possibilities for followers as well as leaders. From the point of view of nonlandowners, an individual has two alternatives. He may join with a leader or he may remain outside the different "fields of authority." If he becomes a follower, he "makes himself subject to the whims of a leader, but profits materially and obtains protection" (1959:69). If he chooses to remain a free agent, he loses material benefits and protection against aggression. A nonlandowner is obviously constrained to become a follower, given that he is poor and lacks alternatives for earning a living. Barth thus argues that it is in the best interests of landowners to seek followers and of nonlandowners to choose leaders.

[Having indicated what motivates and constrains both leaders and followers to enter political relationships, Barth analyzes the strategies available to leaders in their competition with one another.[Leaders mobilize supporters into corporate political groups only "in the event of conflicts" (1959:71). The structure of these groups is not specified by normative principles. Rather, they are constructed around a particular leader for a specific conflict. Therefore, [Barth analyzes those Pathan goals that are "objects of strife" (1959:73) or culturally valued ends.]

Among Pathans, the objects of strife are "women" (zin), "gold" (zer), and "land" (zamin). Land is the primary Pathan interest. Gold symbolizes wealth that may be used to acquire the services of others, leading ultimately to the acquisition and retention of land. Women are a source of conflict because they involve the honor of the family and of its men who are responsible for the conduct of sisters and wives. Failure to uphold such honor is thought to invite encroachments in other areas of leadership. Thus, the bases of authority for political leaders are control of the sources of livelihood, the distribution of wealth, and martial valor in defense of family honor. The pursuit of these is the basis for political conflict and shapes the careers of Pathan leaders.

Such careers are determined by the strategies available to leaders for gaining influence over followers. Barth analyzes these strategies in terms of what is and what is not possible to do. For example, since acquiring land is an important political maneuver, Barth enumerates various methods by which leaders can obtain land including inheritance, reward for service, purchase, force, and deception. There are, however, constraints on each of these alternatives. For example, actions that lead to a conflict over land, which Pathans conceptualize as *shar*, are dangerous because they present a leader's opponents with an opportunity to mobilize against him (cf. 1959:76).

[Barth identifies an organizational principle in these strategies of leadership. "There is," he contends (1959:76), "an upper limit to every chief's aggressiveness, since he must always keep the number of his enemies lower than the total force of his following." He bases this principle on his own analysis. It is not a normative statement elicited from informants, although a shrewd chief would likely recognize its accuracy.]

The distribution of wealth is another source of authority for Pathan leaders. Giving gifts and offering hospitality are important ways to attract and hold followers, and Barth lists the ways in which chiefs may generate income, how they may use it, and why it is so important to followers. Again, although cultural concepts are noted, the analysis is primarily organizational in style: the importance of gift giving and hospitality is to be understood in terms of possibilities and constraints. Thus, Barth notes (1959:79), Pathans distinguish between "satisfied men" (*mor sari*) and "hungry men" (*wuge sari*). Chiefs, as dominant landlords, have access to great resources, while tenants are exceedingly poor. Indeed, he estimates that the average tenant earns one twentieth of the income of the smallest chief (cf. 1959:78). This ratio, plus the fact that wealth in the form of grain is perishable, that its amount is greater than can be consumed by the chief's family, and that it cannot easily be transported for sale outside Swat, means that chiefs have resources available to spend on followers and, given their limited opportunities, must distribute them, if they are to realize their value (cf. 1959:80). Tenants, on the other hand, are poor and are dependent for survival on receiving gifts and hospitality, since they too have limited alternatives for employing their labor, a point that Barth makes in discussing the relative inaccessibility of the Swat valley and the isolation of its population (1959:5–6, 80).

Having examined how leaders establish and maintain positions of political authority and form political groups, Barth describes the relationships between such groups as alliances between leaders and the "blocs" (*dela*) they represent (1959:104). These alliances differ in their construction from the political groups they unite. Political groups are based upon the relation between leaders and their followers. Their solidarity derives from the fact that leaders are able, by dispensing or withholding resources, to reward and punish dependents and from their common interests in a shared enterprise. These shared interests and sanctions follow from the Pakhtuns' control of land and its products and from the limited occupational alternatives for nonlandowners. By contrast, alliances are established between leaders who are equals and who do not otherwise have common interests. They are promises of mutual support in the event of conflict and they are formed and broken by public declaration. That they are formed between equals and are easy to establish and break implies that partners in an alliance are bound not by extrinsic constraints, but only by the common strategic advantage that obtains from the relationship.

Barth examines the conditions that facilitate or inhibit alliance formation. For example, the main lines of cleavage within a bloc are those between close patrilineal kinsmen. Since conflicts in Swat are typically over land or crops and involve members of the same unilineal descent group, who are also neighbors, there is tension built into the relationship between agnates. That is, rather than being allies, agnates are potential rivals and enemies. The Pathan term for close collateral agnates, *tarbur*, also "has the connotation of rival, enemy" (1959:109).

However, the tension implicit in Pathan concepts does not always manifest itself in practice and Barth identifies several constraints on political fissioning (cf. 1959:111). The first is the "fact of group opposition." This means that men grow up in one bloc, have their friends in it, define others as enemies, and are reluctant to "abandon established friends and join the enemy." Another constraint is the "necessity of belonging to a politically viable unit," because it is such a unit that provides strength for bargaining in political negotiations. As Barth states: "Tension between collaterals is thus kept within bounds by the tactical advantage of presenting a solid front." Thus, there are "forces" that "counterbalance" the tension, preventing it from becoming points of fission. His interpretation not only explains where and why tensions lead to splitting, but also the factors that maintain balance in the bloc system.

Correspondingly, Barth contends, there is an inverse relationship between the wealth of landowners and their unity. That is, where there are many Pakhtuns and the average holding is small, there descent groups remain politically united. Conversely, where few landowners control much wealth, there is a tendency toward fission. Barth supports this interpretation with demographic data from different areas of the Swat valley. For example, in one area (the Upper Sebujni), where Pakhtuns constitute between one-third and one-half of the population, the Pakhtun descent groups are united, but in others (Thana and parts of Babuzai), where Pakhtuns form less than one-tenth of the population, there "fission frequently occurs between first cousins or even half-brothers" (1959:112). Thus, Barth analyzes the logical implications of the system to depict the conditions under which fission is more or less likely to occur.

To support his contention that this model represents the process of fission and fusion, he explores its implications for the pattern of land redistribution. One result of the conflict predicted between agnates should be the loss of land by some Pakhtuns and concomitant gain by others. If land were not redistributed in this way, and every Pakhtun were to retain his rightful portion of land, then, as the Pakhtun population increased, the portion of any one caste member would decrease so that all Pakhtuns would eventually be impoverished. Such impoverishment, however, does not occur; instead, Barth states, "land has been progressively concentrated in fewer lines and fewer hands" (1959:112). Thus, Barth's analytical procedure is to argue that if the counterbalancing forces or constraints were not operative, then empirically a pattern different from the observable one would be found.

By a similar method, Barth supports his analysis of the balance between blocs. He argues that the absence of one possible pattern essentially supports the accuracy of the model's prediction of another pattern. In this case, the possible elimination of the weaker of the two blocs through steady erosion of its resources, and therefore of its followers, does not occur. Rivals do encroach on one another's land, which leads to the elimination of caste members. If this process were continued unchecked, then one bloc would become dominant and would eliminate the neighboring bloc. But this does not happen. Rather, according to Barth, the accumulation of power is limited by the interests of individual leaders and the logic of their situation.

Thus, when a bloc composed of rival factions grows large enough to withstand and even dominate its opposition, leaders of these factions break off and go over to the other bloc. Presumably, the seceding leader is the weakest of those in the dominant bloc. He can achieve a position of eminence by becoming a leader of the opposition. In theory, the secession is encouraged by those in the weaker alliance, whose encouragement may be seen as a tactic of subversion (cf. 1959:112–13).

Barth sees the persistence of both blocs as confirmation of his interpretation that an equilibrium within the Pathan political system is based on a balance of power between them. Competition over land leads to agnatic conflict which, if unchecked, would run down the system, exhausting the competitors and their resources. The system continues, however, because there is a continual adjustment between leaders, followers, and resources, resulting in a balanced opposition between blocs.

Barth's examination of the principles of balanced opposition within and between blocs takes the perspective of individual leaders and considers the possibilities open to them for exercising leadership. The process of fission and fusion systematically limits the power of any one bloc, thereby maintaining balance between them. Individual leaders, however, may extend their power by using various strategies to engage dependents and allies and by seceding from one bloc to join the other, even while the blocs in which they have been members decline. Such a situation, Barth concludes, would produce an increasingly powerful individual.

That a central authority does not occur supports Barth's analysis of the factors that constrain leaders. He identifies four factors that inhibit the concentration of authority. They are "the equal division of property between sons, the pattern of personal revenge, the difference in the rate of increase of supporters and opponents, and the opposition of other leaders to the acquisition of predominant power by any individual" (1959:125). Through the custom of equal inheritance of property among sons, a man's estate is fragmented, and each son begins his career with limited power. Tactics, such as the use of violence, that are used to acquire land and thus establish and expand a leader's authority, generate their own constraints on that authority through the custom of seeking personal revenge. As Barth notes (1959:125–26):

> the extension of a man's estate inevitably creates a steadily mounting number of persons dedicated to wreak vengeance on him. . . . Thus the more rapidly a man increases his estate and thereby the centralized group under his control, the greater the chance that his career will be cut short. In the segmentary organization, a leader trying to expand the group of persons directly under his control creates opponents more rapidly than he creates supporters.

Thus, the dynamics of gaining power generates obstacles to retaining it. By these principles, balance is built into the acephalous bloc system. As Barth concludes (1959:134): "The balance within the Swat segmentary system is . . . maintained by a process of growth and ultimate fission of the groups led by single leaders, accompanied by defections from one bloc to the other." The organizational principle that produces balanced opposition is depicted not only at the bloc level, but also as it applies to individuals maneuvering within the system.

MODELS OF FEUDING IN TWO MONOGRAPHS: COMPARING ETHNOGRAPHIC ARGUMENTS

The contrast between Barth's organizational perspective and Evans-Pritchard's structural analysis is particularly evident in their interpretations of feuding. Feuding among Swat Pathans and among the Nuer appears to be similar in practice. Both ethnographers state the causes of feuding and who is involved in them. Among Swat Pathans, feuds are caused by: "murder," "fornication or adultery," "grievous bodily harm deliberately caused in a brawl or by attack," and "any other action which in the situation is understood to constitute a major insult" (1959:83). The duty of avenging a murder falls on the "man who inherits the property of the murdered person" or, failing that, any "male agnate related as first paternal cousin to the dead man, or closer" (1959:84). Barth also indicates who may be held responsible for such harm or insults: agnates of the murderer such as his father, brother, son, uncle, or cousin. Among the Nuer, feuds are also caused by homicide, and, similarly, agnatic kin of the victim are responsible for revenge and those of the murderer may be held accountable for the murder. Moreover, among both Pathans and Nuer, the numbers of people in the groups on both sides of such a conflict are increased by the addition of others: by followers and allies in the first case, and by co-villagers, in the second.

Differences in interpreting feuding behavior apparently follow from the application of different analytical frameworks. For example, Barth's placement of his discussion of Pathan culturally valued ends in the overall argument is noteworthy, especially in comparison with Evans-Pritchard's monograph. Nuer "interests" are analytically similar to Pathan "objects of strife": both are ends whose pursuit typically leads to potentially disruptive conflicts. In *The Nuer*, they are presented in the beginning of the ethnography, as part of the formulation of its analytical problem and solution. That is, the pursuit of cattle leads to conflicts that must be regulated so that such interests may be realized; political conventions create a social order that makes that possible. By contrast, Barth discusses them in the context of interpreting the bases of Pathan leadership, since leadership may be gained, lost, or maintained through conflicts generated around the acquisition and defense of such objects. Neither choice of where to introduce the basis of conflict into the ethnography is arbitrary; each reflects the ethnographer's view of its relevance to the overall argument.

Evans-Pritchard and Barth also differ in their interpretations of the function of "feuding." Evans-Pritchard sees the feud as a mechanism for maintaining equilibrium between local communities. He asserts (1940a: 158–59):

> the blood-feud may be viewed as a structural movement between political segments by which the form of the Nuer political system, as we know it, is maintained .... The function of the feud ... is, therefore, to maintain the structural equilibrium between opposed tribal segments which are, nevertheless, politically fused in relation to larger units.

It is a manifestation of the structural principle of segmentary fission and fusion by which ordered anarchy is achieved among the Nuer. For Barth, a feud provides an occasion on which a leader can act to establish or enhance his authority. Its importance, in his view, derives from its role in the way in which leaders build and maintain a following.

Barth argues that a feud occurs not only as a defense of honor but also as a strategy of leadership. He indicates tactics by which chiefs, through feuding, may enhance their prestige and attract followers. It could be read as a handbook of leadership strategems for Swat Pathans, a manual on how to score points in the game of Pathan politics. Thus, if you want to enhance your prestige, build your reputation, and attract followers, do the following. Demonstrate a penchant for violence and impetuousness; act like a tyrant. Do not leave a murder of a kinsman unavenged. Do not permit gossip about the sexual activities of female kin or affines, or failing to suppress it, take revenge against the seducer. Do not permit any serious insult to go unpunished and punish it preferably by blood revenge. Seek revenge in "excess of talion." These rules represent Barth's understanding of the working system; they are organizational, not normative, principles.

There is some evidence to suggest that had Evans-Pritchard adopted an organizational perspective, his interpretation and presentation of the Nuer material would have been similar to Barth's. For example, he states that the "ability to prosecute a feud . . . depends to some extent on the strength of a man's lineage and on his kin relationships" (1940a:156; cf. 167, 169). Thus, it appears that success in engaging in a feud depends on the capacity to mobilize others on one's behalf. However, his segmentary model of how to mobilize such support would be of little use to the antagonists in a feud. First, they would have to figure out who belonged to which segment—not a simple task, given the relativity and situational selection of social identities—and then they would have to hope that those belonging to the right segments would act in accord with the relevant normative rules.

On the other hand, a re-analysis of Evans-Pritchard's ethnography from a Barthian perspective leads to a different interpretation of the strategies available to Nuer for mobilizing support in the event of conflict. For example, we know from The Nuer that when a village acts corporately, it does so under the leadership of a man known as a "bull" or tut (1940a:178). These leaders appear to recruit followers by the same strategies as do Pathan chiefs: dispensing wealth and exhibiting dominant personalities. For example, if a "bull" "is to gain a social reputation he must . . . possess sufficient cows to be able to entertain guests and to attract young kinsmen to reside in his byre" (1940a:179). This is analogous to the Pathan chief's hospitality being distributed through his "men's house." Furthermore, a Nuer "bull" should have many children, have made marriage alliances, have wealth in cattle, exhibit prowess as a warrior, and possess oratorical skills (1940a:180), expectations that are strikingly similar to those for a Pathan chief. Because of these similarities, it is not unreasonable to consider an alternative to Evans-Pritchard's model of Nuer political organization. Thus, local-level politics among the Nuer, as among the Swat Pathans, may be organized in terms of the relations among "leaders" and between "leaders" and "followers." Similarly, Nuer feuds, like Pathan feuds, may offer an opportunity for leaders to demonstrate and enhance their reputations and thereby strengthen their leadership.

The difference between the accounts of the two societies, at the level of local political organization, may be attributable to the frameworks of ethnographic interpretation rather than to details of social reality. The difference in interpretive framework is evident in Evans-Pritchard's assumption, noted above, that a Nuer "village is a political unit in a structural sense, but it has no political organization" (1940a:180) and in Barth's explicit concern with the internal relationships and organization of Pathan political units. This suggests that the organizational principles of political organization may be more similar in the two societies than would appear to be the case, given the description of the bases of order in them. It also suggests that had Barth done the fieldwork in the southern Sudan, his account would have looked more at leaders and followers, each pursuing their individual interests, and might have been entitled *Political Leadership among Nuer*.

Chapter 5

CASES AND CONTEXTS

Ethnographies focusing on different levels of analysis differ in the kinds of questions they ask, in the sorts of interpretations they offer, and in the types of data they provide. This chapter continues to explore the different ways in which ethnographic accounts are constructed, emphasizing now the use of case materials in ethnographic arguments. In this chapter, I draw on ethnographies discussed in previous chapters (including Barth's *Political Leadership among Swat Pathans* and Ortner's *Sherpas Through Their Rituals*) and introduce, as further examples, Bailey's *Tribe, Caste, and Nation* (1960) and Geertz's "Ritual and Social Change: A Javanese Example" (1973e).

CASE ANALYSIS IN POLITICAL LEADERSHIP AMONG SWAT PATHANS

The data included in *Political Leadership* reflect the different levels of analysis that characterize the monograph. As in structural and symbolic ethnographies, Barth analyzes Pathan modes of thought, deriving them from an examination of native concepts and normative rules. When doing organizational analysis, he focuses on opportunities, constraints, and the processes of decision making and the factors that influence them, as he sees them. He

identifies not only the alternatives available to individuals but also the constraints and the values that make intelligible their selection. These analytical factors (that is, goals, cultural categories, social norms, the possibilities
for action and the limits on them) constitute elements in the logic underlying Pathan political organization.

However, the feature that distinguishes Barth's ethnography from
structural and symbolic studies is his use of material depicting observable
activities as evidence for his claims about what people do and about how the
political organization of Swat Pathans works. He presents much of this evidence as "cases" to exemplify and illustrate his points (1959:19, 20, 41, 97,
117-18, 125, 136-38). He also refers to the material as "examples"
(1959:9-10, 76, 83-85, 99, 107, 111, 120, 127-29) and "illustrations"
(1959:34, 35, 59, 60, 71, 83-85, 99, 111, 113, 117, 120). Sometimes he
writes of a "case" or an "example" that "illustrates" the action in question
(1959:97, 99, 111, 117-18, 125). The same descriptive material may be
referred to by different terms (that is, "case," "example," or "illustration").

Moreover, the same term may refer to different sorts of data. For example, he refers to 476 marriages as "cases" that "express" Pathan conceptualization of "caste" and its associated norm of endogamy (1959:19; cf. 37, 40,
41). He also presents as "cases" descriptions of behavior relating to blood
revenge (1959:83-85;136-38), to the functioning of Pakhtun assemblies
(1959:117-18) and to the processes that produce balance between blocs
(1959:112; 125). Not counting the figures on marriages, Barth includes some
twenty instances of action to serve as supporting evidence.

Furthermore, this evidence also varies along other dimensions. Thus,
Barth uses descriptions of past events as well as of actions that occurred at the
time of his fieldwork; he refers to events that he observed and to events that
others observed and have reported to him; and he refers to "apocryphal dia-
logues" (1959:35-36) and to "traditional accounts" (1959:60). Although
many of the cases that Barth introduces in support of his interpretations
involve anonymous individuals (e.g., 1959:117, 137, 138), others name specific men, either figures from the past (e.g., the Badshah and Jamroz Khan;
1959:35, 113-115, 125-128) or Barth's friends and informants (e.g., Aurangzeb
Khan and Nalkot Pacha; 1959:107, 111; 59, 96, 99, 107, 122, 136).

Barth uses such case material to document his interpretation of different facets of Swat Pathan political organization. For example, he presents
five cases that document blood revenge in defense of honor, thereby illustrating his analysis of the ways in which chiefs acquire and maintain authority and leadership (1959:81-86; 136-38). In one case, two murders are committed in retaliation for one. In another, a man is killed and the victim's
nephew (Nalkot Pacha) not only kills the murderer but also destroys the
crops of the supporters of the murderer and requires them to beg for forgive-

ness. The following is the text of the case of Nalkot Pacha (1959:136):

> *Sayyid of Biha vs. Pacha of Nalkot: Saints of two neighboring villages in upper Sebunji, c. 1925.*
>
> The Sayyid of Biha reaped fodder from a certain G.M.'s fields; he was surprised and beaten by G.M. and his skull was fractured. People egged him on, teasing him for having been beaten, and that by a man so short of stature as G.M. The Sayyid therefore surprised G.M. once in Biha and beat him with the aid of fellow villagers. G.M. then wanted revenge; he waited by the part in the valley bottom, managed to catch two of the Sayyids, and tried to shame them by removing their trousers. In self-defense the Sayyid of Biha slashed G.M.'s stomach open with a knife; he was then caught and tied up. Next morning G.M. died. His son was still a child, and his adult close agnates did not dare take revenge. The more distant relatives were offered the chance of revenge, but hesitated on the ground that they were not closely enough related. So Nalkot Pacha, the brother's son of the murdered man, shot the captive murderer. Later Khan Bahadur Sahib supported Nalkot Pacha's group; they raided Biha and burnt the Sayyid's crops, but the Sayyids had fled to Dir. After three years they returned on the Night of Sacrifice, and begged pardon of the family, which was then granted.

In these cases, a show of superiority not only repairs the damage and reestablishes prestige, but it also increases the reputation of a leader by providing evidence for his claims to authority.

Barth uses two other cases, also involving Nalkot Pacha, to depict the political roles of saints. One illustrates the way in which symbols of saintly status can be manipulated for political purposes. He claims (1959:59) that in their position as mediators, saints conventionally wear a "white turban which makes them inviolable in feud, and permits them to cross from one warring camp to the other." He also notes that "this privilege does not, however, prevent them carrying arms at other times," adding that Nalkot Pacha has been faced with "dilemma of choice, at critical moments in his career, between arms and the white turban, and even of the quick change from one to the other in the middle of battle" (1959:59). The other case illustrates the way in which a saint may use "both holy status and force" to "enlarge his field of manoeuvre" (1959:99):

> Two opposed persons from different communities were to meet with the Pacha on the border between the territories, so that he could make a settlement. One man came as instructed, alone and unarmed. The

other brought a considerable armed party. The unarmed man sought cover behind the Pacha, the other party edged around them and were planning to execute the man before the Pacha, thereby forcing him to save face by pretending this had been his verdict, or else admit that he had been outwitted. But the Pacha put his fingers in his mouth and whistled, whereupon his own men, who had concealed themselves in the area several hours before the time set for the meeting, rose and converged on the breakers of the truce. These latter thereupon threw down their arms and begged the Pacha's forgiveness—so he settled the conflict on fair terms.

Barth notes that these accounts of "turban switching" and "secreted men" are examples of "practical politics" (1959:99), the very sort of actions that Evans-Pritchard largely overlooked in his analysis of the normative rules guiding Nuer political relationships.

Barth's organizational perspective is particularly evident in two other cases illustrating the tactics and strategies that produce balance between blocs. Both concern the alignment of leaders within a bloc, focusing on the processes of rivalry and secession. Barth presents a model of this process, as noted above. He posits that in the conflict between blocs, one bloc, at any given time, dominates the other. This enables its members to exploit those of the opposition, taking their land and thereby further controlling them. Logically, this should lead to the demise of the weaker bloc. This, however, does not happen, because rivalries between allies within the dominant bloc lead one or another faction to secede from it to the other weaker bloc.

To illustrate the working of this model, Barth provides case evidence. It exemplifies, as he states, the "recent history of the chiefs of Maruf khel, Babuzai as given by numerous informants of both blocs" (1959:113):

> The opposition in this area in the last century was between Malak Baba of Maruf khel and the chief of Juna khel. Malak Baba nearly exterminated the Juna khel, establishing himself as leader of the dominant bloc and meanwhile increasing his private property from four to fifty shares (Rupei) of land. Upon his death, disagreement over succession and inheritance led to fission between his sons. Nowsherawan Kaka succeeded his father, and Jamroz Khan seceded from the bloc with his full brothers, his half brother Janes Kaka, and all their followers, to join the remains of the Juna khel and become their leader. There was, incidentally, never an ordered division of the estate of Malak Baba. Each group of sons seized the fields in the area controlled by their party; but at the subsequent re-allotments each brother had a legal right to one eleventh of the father's fifty shares. Jamroz Khan

joined an alliance with the Mianguls (the Badshah, later founder of Swat State, and his brother Shirin Sahib . . .) and his party dominated the Babuzai area; but when the Badshah and Shirin Sahib later became estranged, Jamroz Khan supported the latter, whereas the party of the former, supported by Nowsherawan Kaka, came into power. Shirin Sahib was later killed in battle. Later on, as Nowsherawan Kaka's bloc grew in strength and threatened to become independent of Badshah's support, the latter abandoned him and joined the other bloc. They arranged the murder of Jamroz Khan, supporting Pir Mohammed Khan (Jamroz Khan's half-brother's son) as the local leader of their bloc. This led to a split between Pir Mohammed Khan and the sons of Jamroz Khan and his full brothers who broke away under Aurangzeb Khan.

A second case about assembly tactics and strategies also illustrates the principle underlying balanced opposition between blocs on which Swat Pathan political organization is based as well as the ways in which individuals circumvent the norms that are supposed to govern their behavior. Although Barth states that it is an actual case, I will identify the two protagonists as "A" and "B," since Barth acknowledges that the names he uses are "fictitious" (1959:117).

At the time of the incident A and B were leaders in their respective blocs. An ally of A was using the land in question, claiming to have obtained the right to do so from its owner, before the latter died. The other leader, B, an agnate of the dead man, brought his dependents' claims for the land to the assembly for a decision. He employed a variety of tactics to rally support. He caucused with his allies to solidify the backing of his own bloc. He consulted with members of the other bloc, attempting to encourage rivalry among them in order to divide them and thereby reduce the strength of the opposition. He called in a favor from an opposition member, who had once been an ally, to further neutralize the opposition's strength. He successfully bargained for the betrayal of its leader by one member of the opposing bloc who was seeking to gain for himself control of the bloc.

Leader A also used a number of tactics to defend his case, actions based on the cultural rules about the equality of members of the assembly. He exhorted others to not find in B's favor, since, he implied, to do so would make them B's dependents and not his equals. When that appeal made little impact, he resorted to interrupting a speaker, claiming that the latter was inferior to the other members of the assembly. This attempt to silence a member of the opposition violated the norm that all members had the right to address the assembly, and allowed B to bring a charge of contempt against A. A was fined for this flagrant violation of the norms regarding assembly behavior (which his dependent paid), but the furor over this infraction distracted attention from the discussion at hand. Consequently, there was no resolution of the dispute, at least at that moment. Thus, the land remained in the use of A's ally.

Barth holds that this type of evidence warrants his interpretation of Swat political organization. He states (1959:118):

> Such tactical manoeuvres, designed to protect the interests of allies and the strength of the bloc as a whole, are characteristic of assembly activities; and specialized skill in such manoeuvres is a highly valued attribute of leaders. This constant emphasis on the interests and advantage of allies prevents us from regarding the assemblies as governing bodies, and analyzing the extent of their authority and the field of their activity. The empirical facts force us to give primary attention to the organization into blocs and the principles of rivalry and balanced opposition on which this organization is based, and to regard the assembly meetings as merely one institutionalized field in which these principles are expressed.

[Barth's use of such case materials to document analysis of actual behavior, especially of the choices that individuals make in pursuing their interests, marks a departure from studies that emphasize the systematization of a people's cultural concepts and normative rules. Other monographs develop this style of ethnography even further.]

CASE ANALYSIS IN TRIBE, CASTE, AND NATION

F. G. Bailey, in *Tribe, Caste, and Nation* (1960), like Firth and Barth, examines the possibilities of action, but extends the implementation of an organizational perspective by focusing even more closely on the process in terms of which people choose among alternative courses of action. This leads him to consider the particular characteristics of a specific individual's situation as among those factors that influence his choices. Barth presents cases—incidences of actual behavior—in support of his claims about the dynamics of Swat Pathan political organization, employing them to illustrate actions taken by individuals acting within a context of structural principles and environmental constraints. Bailey also uses case material in this way, but he takes the methodology a step further by presenting and analyzing case material to examine the processes of decision making. He considers not only what people do, but also the alternatives not chosen, the conditions under which choices are and are not made, and the implications of choosing one or another course of action (including its costs and benefits, advantages and disadvantages), as seen by the actors—those involved in the actions—as well as by the analyst-ethnographer.

Bailey interprets cases contextually, although he argues that what constitutes a context is a problematic aspect of ethnographic description and is itself an object of analysis. For example, some ethnographers interpret behavior within a context that is defined in terms of a single ideational system. Thus, Barth examines action within a single cultural framework, that of Swat Pathans' values, concepts, and norms about what should and can be done in political activities, although he is attentive to nonnormative influences on behavior. Other ethnographers interpret behavior in contexts that are characterized by several different standards for evaluating action. For example, Leach, in *Political Systems of Highland Burma*, argues that Kachin claims about their actions and those of others only make sense in terms of the contrasting ideational models they hold, that of a political doctrine of aristocracy (*gumsa*) or that of democracy (*gumlao*). Bailey's monograph integrates these approaches to ethnography. He demonstrates that certain actions or events, presented as cases, can be understood only by placing them within a context defined by different structures or cultural frameworks.

Bailey's ethnography illustrates the complexity of analyzing case material in such contexts. He describes an event and interprets it in terms of the structures within which it is located. These structures are the context of the case. However, this context is itself the product of analysis and interpretation. In this sense, an event or case can be viewed as a window through which an ethnographer can present (and a reader can grasp) the context (society, culture) in which it occurs. As Bailey puts it: "Events in the village provide a text, in the commentary upon which the wider systems are unfolded" (1960: 269; cf. 225). It is important to note, however, that such a presentation of an event is a heuristic device for the anthropologist who is writing the ethnography and that it is the anthropologist who, working on several levels of analysis and using different types of data beyond those of the case itself, ultimately interprets and describes those wider systems. (See Pitt-Rivers 1967 and Gellner 1970 for a discussion of the analytical and interpretive implications of the ways in which ethnographers determine the boundaries of a context and of a case—or a concept—that is located within it.) In short, context is used to make intelligible the meaning of a case and a case is used to illuminate the context in which it occurs.

This view of the relationship between case and context informs Bailey's description of political activity in a village in the Kond Hills of highland Orissa in eastern India. He describes three political structures that constitute the context of the events he analyzes. These structures are the political system of the Konds, the indigenous tribal people of the area who traditionally were organized in a segmentary lineage system; the caste system of the Oriyas, Hindus who entered the highlands from the surrounding plains; and the rules and regulations of the administration, first that of the British colonial government and then that of the independent Indian government. Each of these structures are based on, and defined in terms of, cultural concepts and normative rules that are different from one another. Yet, because they co-exist, they define alternative courses of action. Bailey focuses on the ways in which people in one setting, that of the village of Baderi, respond, and fail to respond, to the different possibilities of action that these structures provide.

The textual organization of *Tribe, Caste, and Nation* reflects Bailey's argument about data and interpretation. The monograph is divided into three parts. The first two parts, representing almost three-quarters of the ethnography, depict the different structures that shape political activity in the village: the tribal system of the Konds, caste relationships among Konds and Oriyas, and the administration of the government district in which the village is situated. The third part presents an analysis of political activity within the context of these multiple structures: it consists of a description of a single "case" and the ethnographer's interpretation of it. Using this case, Bailey analyzes the actions of individuals in terms of the opportunities and constraints afforded by these different structures. He describes the ways in which individuals use and manipulate one structure in relation to another, focusing on these possibilities and on those who respond to them.

The case that Bailey selects to illustrate his argument centers on a dispute between Konds and Oriyas that occurred in Baderi village at the time that he was doing fieldwork there. An account of the case was written for him by the local schoolmaster, an Oriya who lives in another village in the district, who was himself involved in the dispute. The informant's text consists of approximately two-and-a-half pages in the monograph, although Bailey's analysis of it takes another thirty-seven pages, constituting the remainder of the chapter.

Bailey summarizes the dispute as follows (1960:200):

> A minor Government functionary seems to have attempted to embezzle a small sum. This alleged peculation was detected. Another man, not directly concerned in the matter, being drunk and uninhibited, made use of it to say what he thought about various individuals and categories of persons, both those who had offended and those who in this case were free from blame.

As Bailey relates the story, there are five principle people involved in the dispute. These are (1) *Nrusingh*, an Oriya, who is the minor Government functionary (a *paik* or administrative assistant) who attempted the embezzlement; (2) *Goneswaro*, also an Oriya, Nrusingh's superior and the *sirdar* or head of the administrative division (*mutha*) in which the village is located; (3) *Manda*, a Kond, and the victim of the embezzlement; (4) *Liringa*, a Kond, a resident of the village who attempted to support Manda; and (5) *Ponga*, a Kond, headman of the village, and the drunk who abused everybody.

The basic actions in the case are as follows. Nrusingh, assistant to the head of the administrative division in which Baderi village is located, came to the village to collect taxes. He received, as partial payment, a certain sum of money from Manda. When Nrusingh turned that payment over to Goneswaro, the administrative head, he gave an amount less than that which Manda had given to him. The next day, Goneswaro noted that Manda owed a balance, based on the lesser amount reported to him by Nrusingh. Manda protested that he paid more. Liringa, a resident of Baderi, intervened to say that he was present when Manda paid Nrusingh and the payment was in the amount indicated by Manda. Liringa demanded that Goneswaro write either a receipt for the full amount paid or a statement that he had received a lesser amount from his assistant, Nrusingh. Goneswaro declined to write either, saying that he would talk with his assistant about the matter. Nrusingh returned to Baderi on the following day, this time in his role as a trader to buy some tumeric from Ponga, the headman of Baderi village. When Ponga, who was drunk at the time, saw Nrusingh enter the village, he went into a rage and began to berate Nrusingh for having cheated Manda. Then Ponga turned his abusive attention to others, finally beating his own son and kicking him out of his house. The son went to stay with his spiritual advisor, a Hindu, with whom he returned to Baderi the next day, when the latter forbade Ponga to drink and Ponga agreed not to do so again. This ended the incident.

Bailey interprets the actions of these individuals in terms of "different social systems" (in this case, the multiple structures of tribe, caste, and nation) in which people have "roles to play" (1960:211). Thus, the analysis of "roles," the culturally defined expectations about and possibilities for behavior, and the structures in which they are embedded, link Bailey's interpretation of decision making and the actors who make decisions. For example, Nrusingh, the man who attempted the alleged embezzlement, plays several roles and therefore has alternatives for action defined by different structures. He is an Oriya of untouchable caste and a client (*proja*) of Goneswaro, who is an Oriya of higher caste. He is also a *paik*, an administrative assistant, to Goneswaro in the latter's role as *sirdar* or administrative head of the district. For Nrusingh and Goneswaro the roles of client in the caste system and assistant in the administration are complementary: in both systems, "Goneswaro gives the orders and Nrusingh obeys" (1960:201). However, Nrusingh has other roles that are not so simply reconciled. He is also a wealthy trader and his "standing as a man of substance is in contradiction to his roles as an untouchable and as the client of Goneswaro" (1960:201). This contradiction is part of the complexity of the relationships that constitute the context of the incident.

Nrusingh's actions also are considered from the additional perspective of his relationship with the Konds of Baderi. As an untouchable, even though an Oriya, he ranks lower than the Konds who are considered of clean caste and therefore of higher status. By custom, he should behave in ways that express deference toward them. On the other hand, he is an administrative assistant, a representative of the government, and he has some authority, of which he takes advantage to act superior toward the Konds who are considered his superordinates in the caste structure. The relationship between Nrusingh and the Konds is complicated even further by the implicit superiority of Oriyas in general over Konds. With this superiority in mind, Nrusingh is seen, Bailey states, "as a representative—in Kond eyes a poor representative—of the culture and civilization towards which the . . . Konds are striving" (1960:206). Finally, Nrusingh is a trader and is the middleman between the Konds who grow tumeric and the merchants who buy it.

Thus, Nrusingh occupies a position in which he has several alternatives for action, each of which can influence the other. He is able to use his role as an official and as a trader to offset the disabilities associated with his role as an untouchable. He also uses his status as an Oriya to exploit his relationship with the Konds, including the man whom he tried to embezzle. The various roles of Nrusingh create a situation of ambiguity in which structures and individuals can be manipulated. Bailey summarizes the situation (1960:208–209):

> Neither in his relationships with the Sirdar, nor in his relationship with the Konds, is Nrusingh playing a single unitary role, within one structure of social relations. In both cases Nrusingh operates in two or more social systems. To the Sirdar he is at once an untouchable client, a junior official, and a relatively well-to-do entrepreneur. To the Konds he is a PAN [an untouchable], an Oriya PAN, an official and a trader. To each of these roles is attached an appropriate form of behavior: that is to say, in the case of Nrusingh and the Konds, he may behave as PAN, an offical, or a trader; and conversely the Konds may treat him as any one of these three, but not all three at the same time, because the roles are in some situations contradictory. For instance the greeting to an official is not also the appropriate greeting to an

untouchable, for the one demonstrates inferiority and the other superiority. In every situation the actors have an element of latitude and may choose the way they will behave in order to further their own ends. The Konds can humiliate Nrusingh by treating him as an untouchable or they can flatter him by treating him as an official, whichever suits their purpose. There is no single system into which can be placed all the relationships in which Nrusingh is concerned. Rather there are a number of alternative systems, from which people can choose how they will behave.

Bailey interprets Nrusingh's behavior in just these terms. He states (1960:206): "Nrusingh's ... attempt to appropriate part of the tax money is not simply an attempt to cheat the Government, but is also an extension of the normal behavior of an [untouchable] in monetary dealings with Konds." Here Bailey analyzes Nrusingh's behavior as that of an educated Oriya exploiting an illiterate Kond. Moreover, he sees that Nrusingh's position is strengthened by his measure of independence from his master, Goneswaro. Nrusingh is in a strong position because, as a relatively wealthy trader, he has an alternative to the clientship associated with his low-caste status, thereby freeing him somewhat from the sanctions that could otherwise compel him to behave in the deferential way expected of a client. Hence, the anthropologist sees Nrusingh's action as stemming both from his structural positions as well as from his ability and willingness to use these different roles to advance his own interest.

Bailey also interprets Goneswaro's actions in terms of structural alternatives. As he does with Nrusingh, he focuses on the multiplicity of structures and the opportunities they imply for Goneswaro. For example, he asks (1960:202) about Goneswaro, "what were the courses open to the Sirdar," and proceeds to describe them. Goneswaro, Bailey hypothesizes, might have given a receipt for the incomplete amount he received from his assistant, but that had its drawbacks. It would expose the inefficiency of his administration or it might expose him to a charge of embezzlement, if his assistant was able to persuade others that he had in fact handed over the full amount of tax to his superior. Alternatively, Goneswaro might have given a receipt for the full amount of the tax, but "this might set a precedent for dishonest Konds" (1960:202), and he would have the problem of getting Nrusingh to pay him the difference or of paying it himself. Bailey makes clear the basis for the choice made by considering, and discounting, the alternatives available to the individuals involved in the action. In the case of the attempted embezzlement, he contextualizes action by comparing what an individual did with what he could have done.

Similarly, Bailey assesses Manda's behavior in terms of the alternative courses of action open to him. According to the ethnographer, there were three possible ways in which the victim of the attempted embezzlement could have behaved, each reflecting one of the structures that shapes local life (1960:217–19). As a citizen, Manda could have sought relief in the government court in which he would have had equal status with Nrusingh and Goneswaro. As a subordinate, he could have appealed to Goneswaro, attempting to remind the *sirdar* of his responsibility to protect his dependents. Finally, Manda could have attempted to rally his fellow Konds to pressure the *sirdar*, uniting tribesmen against the Oriya outsider, to resolve the case to his satisfaction. Bailey notes that these alternatives were not mutually exclusive; he also suggests that Manda relied upon the middle course, presumably because the possible costs of litigation and of providing for his co-villagers would have outweighed the benefits of a legal victory.

The influence of multiple structures is evident also in the behavior of Liringa, the bystander who intervened on behalf of Manda. Bailey interprets Liringa's actions not as those of a man simply helping a fellow villager, but rather in terms of the options provided by the situation as these relate to Liringa's efforts to advance his own interests. That is, Liringa is attempting to play off one system against another, taking advantage of the different courses of action defined by the different rules or structures. In this sense, Bailey sees the conflict between Konds and Oriyas as well as the competition within the Kond political system as the context for Liringa's intervention.

Thus, Liringa supported Manda and verbally attacked Goneswaro to advance his own claim to leadership of the Konds in Baderi village. He was able to take advantage of the conflict between an administrative head and the people in his district, and between an Oriya and a Kond, to advance himself. In other words, Liringa, in competition with the headman of the village, Ponga, tried to gain in that tribal structure by reacting to a situation created by the existence of administrative and caste structures. As Bailey states (1960:223): "Liringa was able to make use of a dispute which arose in the system of relationships between Kond and Oriya, and between a Sirdar and his subjects, in order to strengthen his own position against a rival in quite a different system, the political system of a Kond." Liringa's behavior, like that of Nrusingh, Goneswaro, and Manda, is to be understood from the perspective of the alternatives defined not only within a structure but also between structures.

Bailey also interprets Ponga's behavior in terms of the roles that are available to him. Ponga is subordinate to Goneswaro as a village headman in the administrative system and as a Kond in the caste system. However, within the same administrative structure, Ponga represents his fellow Kond villagers. Moreover, he sells tumeric and is in a trading relationship with Nrusingh, which, Bailey suggests, he might have used to help Manda and to resist Liringa's efforts to subvert his own standing in the tribal system. That Ponga failed to take action in any of these roles does not undermine Bailey's analysis of the possibilities; rather, it indicates, as Bailey notes, that personal capacities and inclinations of the actors—the people the ethnographer is describing—also must be considered in interpreting their behavior.

Consequently, Bailey incorporates into his analysis assessments of the character and personal history of the individuals whose choices he is trying to understand. Thus, the ethnographer describes how these factors influence the ways in which Goneswaro handles the options available to him, and, correspondingly, the ways in which these shape his relationships with others. He writes (1960:209–10):

> I have neither the training nor the knowledge to make anything more than superficial comment on Goneswaro's character. However, his character is clearly of importance and I must take account of it in my arguments. . . . I shall assume that Goneswaro's success or failure within the limits set by social factors is the result of his personality, which my analysis must take as given.
>
> The signs of incapacity as a leader are obvious enough, once one gets past Goneswaro's patriarchal appearance. He has a bad stammer. He cannot speak well in a meeting . . . [He] is an old man, crippled by rheumatism: he walks with a stick and is frequently unable to walk at all. He is unable to visit his *mutha* [district] frequently and he has to rely on his *paik* [assistant] Nrusingh. . . . Goneswaro's life has been . . . a failure. He is a member and could be the head of a large and wealthy lineage . . . but he has quarreled with his collaterals so many times that he has little influence. He has no son, a sure sign that he was born under an unfavorable star.

Bailey sees that these personal weaknesses influence Goneswaro's actions and those who interact with him.

Although some individuals attempt to use one role to offset as far as possible the disadvantages of another or to use it to take advantage of still another role, Goneswaro does not. Thus, Goneswaro, as *sirdar*, is expected to travel through his district, but his physical infirmity limits him and makes his dependent on his assistant, Nrusingh, a situation that the latter does use to his own advantage. In the same way, Goneswaro's infirmity influences his relationship with those Konds who are under his authority. Konds are supposed to show respect toward their *sirdar*, but since Goneswaro lacks the ability or the will to enforce the sanctions associated with his role, they do not accord him deference. This, Bailey argues, explains why Goneswaro was abused by Liringa.

Similarly, Bailey describes the personal characteristics of the other protagonists in his story. For example, Bailey writes of the victim (1960:217):

> Manda Kohoro is a young man, slightly corpulent for a Kond, with a puffiness about the eyes and cheeks that is a sign of internal disorders caused by protracted malaria. He is frequently ill, and this may be the reason why his fields are not well cultivated and he is reputed to be a slovenly farmer. He is occasionally taken by a fit, and he has acquired the reputation as a diviner and a healer. He is well-to-do, as standards are in Baderi, in spite of his poor cultivation. He is also shy, quietly spoken, and is considered a friendly, inoffensive person, but not a fool. It may have been his docility, combined with a slight affluence, that caused Nrusingh to choose him as the victim of his peculations.

And he writes of Liringa, who, standing up for the victim, confronted Goneswaro, the *sirdar* (1960:220–21):

> Liringa intervened in a way that was characteristic of him. He avoided the uninhibited and self-destroying frenzy of Ponga: but he struck more sharply and decisively on Manda's behalf than did Manda himself. His aggression was calculated not only to disturb Goneswaro and to voice the inarticulate feelings of the Konds around him, but also to enhance his own position among the Konds of Baderi. By serving one end he could also serve the other: the two aims, in other words, although in two different social systems, were complementary: and Liringa made use of his opportunities, neither underplaying them nor overplaying them. . . . Liringa's intervention was the more disturbing to Goneswaro because he knew that not only was Liringa a more determined, a more resourceful, and an altogether tougher person than Manda, but also because he was much more capable of carrying out his threats than any other Kond in Baderi. He is a man of about forty, ambitious in village politics, shrewd, and very articulate, but without the wealth and lacking that blundering charisma which keeps Ponga in the first position in the village. . . . He can present a case with force and clarity, and had the matter come before the Revenue Inspector, it would have been Liringa, and not Manda himself or the village headman Ponga, who would have spoken against Goneswaro and Nrusingh. As advocates neither Nrusingh nor Goneswaro could have matched him in debate, and both Goneswaro and Liringa himself knew this.

In these statements, as well as in other parts of his account, Bailey interprets an action, or a failure to act, in terms of information known or knowable to particular actors. However, the actors may or may not see the alternatives in the same way. Sometimes the analyst presents the possible courses of action as if an actor were cognizant of them and weighed the costs and benefits of each before acting. For example, Bailey states (1960:206):

> Nrusingh probably hoped that Manda would not—or could not—read what was on the receipt. There are, of course, other factors which might have entered into his calculations: the lax system of accounting; his strong position against the Sirdar . . . and the possibility that even if he were discovered, then the worst that could happen would be that he would have to make good what he had taken.

Whether or not Nrusingh hoped or calculated, as Bailey states he probably did, the alternatives are ones that the ethnographer has sorted out.

In still other examples, it is explicitly stated that it is the ethnographer who sees the options. For instance, after describing the ways in which Manda could have behaved, including either complaining to a magistrate as a wronged citizen or invoking the support of his fellow Konds to pressure Goneswaro, Bailey writes (1960:219), "I do not think that Manda had worked all this out step by step as I have written it." This is not to say that such a perspective is not or could not be held by an actor in the situation; rather, it underscores the point that such alternatives are analytical constructions, used by the writer to make sense of observable actions.

Just as the ethnographer presents information about the actors' lives to make sense of their behavior in a particular incident, he also draws on knowledge of relationships and conditions external to the incident itself in constructing his account of it. That is, Bailey's interpretation of the case depends on his access to and analysis of data that pertain to, and were collected in, circumstances beyond those evident in the text of the attempted embezzlement. For example, Bailey assesses the Konds' reactions to Goneswaro by comparing their treatment of their *sirdar* with that of the people in the neighboring administrative unit. He argues that Konds expect, among other things, their *sirdar* to intercede on behalf of his subjects with officials, that he protect them from outsiders, and that he settle disputes among them. Given these expectations, and Goneswaro's failure to meet them, the Konds' attitude of contempt toward Goneswaro is understandable. By contrast, the Konds of the adjacent administrative unit were afraid of their *sirdar* because they feared him as a man. "Goneswaro," Bailey writes (1960:212), "with exactly the same formal powers, and the same structural position in the society, they came near to despising." The normative rules governing the role behavior of a *sirdar* and his relationship with his subjects constitute background information for understanding the case in question:

they are the cultural standards in terms of which behavior is intelligible.

Bailey explicitly describes how he acquired such material. In referring to the Konds' view of the exemplary relationship between themselves and subjects, he states (1960:213): "In Balimendi [the administrative division in which the village of Baderi is located] I have taken part in discussions about whom the Konds should choose to succeed Goneswaro. . . . It was in these discussions that I learnt what kind of personality the ideal Sirdar should have and what duties he should undertake." Bailey also notes other information regarding the *sirdar* and/or the Konds that was gained from sources external to the drama that he is analyzing: he refers to his observations of councils at which the *sirdar* presided (1960:213), his conversations with a Revenue Inspector (1960:216) and with Liringa (1960:223), and the "standard complaints" of Konds regarding the misuse of political authority by Oriyas (1960:232). In short, Bailey's analysis and description of the case entails his grasp of the wider cultural context in which it occurs, a context that he abstracts from behavior that is extrinsic to the case.

Bailey's analysis of the incident of the attempted embezzlement illustrates the complexity of interpreting ethnographic data, his similarity to other styles of presenting ethnography, as well as the ways in which he has moved beyond them. The foundation of Bailey's ethnography is structural analysis—the depiction of rules of behavior. Thus, Bailey establishes each of the structures of political action (tribe, caste, and nation) with reference to their standards of conduct and the meaning of behavior within them. However, he extends that mode of ethnography by focusing on the relationship between ideas and action. Many ethnographers acknowledge that there is a difference between what is expected and what actually happens. Bailey utilizes that recognition and develops his analysis by concentrating on such discrepancies in his explanation of people's behavior. His use of case material illustrates that perspective.

CASE ANALYSIS IN SYMBOLIC ETHNOGRAPHY

The analysis and presentation of case material is characteristic of ethnographic studies of modes of action. It does not follow, however, that cases must be used in this way or that anthropologists who focus on modes of thought do not present similar kinds of data. An examination of examples of symbolic ethnography illustrates the point that although anthropologists writing different kinds of ethnographies use cases, they use them in quite different ways. Moreover, the description and analysis of case material in organizational and symbolic ethnographies exemplify a crucial difference between them. Both types of ethnography incorporate examples of social interaction, in contrast to structural studies that delineate normative rules and that are characterized by a paucity of data regarding what people actually do. In organizational ethnographies, these events are typically identified as "cases." In symbolic ethnographies too, they are presented as "cases," but also as "incidents," "representative anecdotes," "cultural performances," or "texts." The concern in both organizational and symbolic ethnographies is to understand a case in terms of the context in which it occurs, to interpret the meaning of an event by placing it within a wider setting. The types of ethnography differ in how they define and document a context and therefore in the way in which they attribute meaning to a "case" and the behavior it depicts.

In organizational ethnographies, like Bailey's *Tribe, Caste, and Nation*, context includes environmental and normative constraints, the latter presented in terms of normative principles and legal rules. Context also incorporates the opportunities available to individuals in particular situations by virtue of the overlapping of multiple structures, each representing an alternative course of action. Moreover, organizational ethnographers examine the past experiences and personal dispositions of the individuals involved in the case in order to show how these too shape their present behavior. Taken together, these factors provide the background for the case within which actions of individuals are interpreted. The analyst looks not only at what happens, but also at what might have happened, since behavior is not simply or directly determined by any single structure, and individuals could have behaved differently than they did.

In symbolic ethnography, case material is handled quite differently. This difference is evident in Geertz's interpretation of a Javanese funeral, "Ritual and Social Change: A Javanese Example" (1973e), published two years before Barth's monograph and one year before Bailey's. It is an example, as he describes it, of "ritual failure" (1973e:146). The case involves the death of a young boy and the disruptions that occurred in the usual pattern of completing a funeral shortly after death. Instead of a "calm, undemonstrative, almost languid letting go" (1973e:153), this particular funeral was marked by delay, by tension among those who attended it, and by an uncharacteristic display of emotion on the part of the mourners.

To understand the event and its failure to unfold as it should have, Geertz presents the conceptual structures within which the funeral would ordinarily have made sense. That is, he describes Javanese values, concepts, and norms concerning death and the ways in which the living expect and are expected to deal with it. The description is complicated by the fact that in this particular case two different cultural systems provided different guidelines for action and for interpreting the meaning of the event. These two cultural systems were, in turn, associated with different categories of people, representing different political ideologies. One was associated with *santris* who emphasized the performance of pure Islamic ritual and who favored an Islam-based political party (Masjumi). The other was associated with *abangans* who emphasized secular rituals, informed by a combination of non-Islamic, Marxist, and nativist ideas, and who preferred an anti-Moslem political group (Permai). Geertz describes these two frameworks, since it is with reference to them that he interprets the case of the disrupted funeral.

Geertz also describes the funeral in some detail. The case revolves around the burial of a young boy, who had been living with his aunt and uncle in a small town. As is the Javanese custom, the boy was supposed to have been buried within a few hours after death by the religious official (a *modin*) responsible for conducting funerals. In fact, the funeral did not take place in the usual manner, the burial coming only after many hours' delay, a delay precipitated by the religious official's refusal to participate in the ritual. Geertz relates that refusal and the disruption it caused to the conflict between *santris* and *abangans*. When the boy died, his uncle sent word to the boy's parents and to the *modin*. The *modin*, who was also a local Masjumi leader, arrived at the uncle's house and noticed a Permai political poster. He then told the uncle that he could not perform the ritual since the uncle belonged to another religion for which he, the religious official, being a Moslem, did not know the correct ritual. There followed a series of actions, each contributing to a growing tension among the uncle's neighbors, who, although of different religious and political persuasions, were traditionally obligated to participate in the funeral process, including the communal feast (*slametan*), which marked the end of the ritual. The tension was finally alleviated and the ritual process resumed when one man, who, although a *santri* and a member of Masjumi, was also a close neighbor of the uncle, encouraged other *santris* to take up their part in the funeral ritual. This intervention was strengthened by the arrival of the dead boy's father, who said that although not very religious and a member of neither political party, he wanted his son to be buried in the Islamic way, a procedure that he contrasted with Christian custom. At that point, the *modin*, with the assistance of several *santris*, buried the body, reciting the appropriate final words, thereby bringing the funeral to an end.

Geertz's interpretation of this event emphasizes the goal of understanding behavior in terms of a cultural system, focusing on the concepts, norms, and values that give meaning to action and on the confusion characterizing an event, in this case a funeral, which follows when two different cultural systems, frameworks of interpretation, are applied to it. Thus, he concludes (1973e:165) that the "disorganization of the ritual resulted from a basic ambiguity in the meaning of the rite for those who participated in it." In Geertz's view, the problem is a confusion over the meaning of the event (that is, whether the funeral is a religious or a political event), and he argues that the conflict is to be understood by identifying and sorting out the different conceptual structures implicated in it.

For this case, Geertz examines the systems, but not the individuals who choose between different possible courses of action. He does not regard the actions of individuals as decisions, although clearly each person had alternatives, nor does he question closely how a particular decision to act is related to an individual's past, present, or probable future experiences and/or interests. It is not that data of that sort are not included in the description, but rather that they are not emphasized analytically.

An ethnographer presenting an organizational analysis of the funeral conflict would probably include more information about the actors, the opportunities available to them, and their relationships with one another. For example, he would point out that the religious functionary (the *modin*), having noticed the poster with its symbol of the political opposition, had a choice of ignoring it or commenting upon it and would question what factors led to his choosing to respond to it as he did. This, in turn, would lead to an account of village politics and of the particular political relationships (as well as other types of relationships) that obtain between the actors. Was the *santri* mediator in competition with the *modin* for local leadership in the Masjumi political party? Was the *modin* using this incident to advance not only his political party but also his personal interests? What was the economic interest of the *modin* and how was it related to those of the shopkeeper uncle and the tailor/mediator? Questions of this type, characteristic of an organizational ethnography, address not only the existence and import of cultural systems, but also the ways in which individuals respond to and manipulate those systems and the factors that shape their ability and willingness to do so. In an organizational study, context is construed not only as ideas and beliefs, but also as personalities and opportunities. In symbolic ethnographies, the emphasis in on symbols and their meanings.

This emphasis is also evident in "Thick Description" (1973b), Geertz's description of a "mock sheep raid," involving a conflict among Berber horsemen, Jewish peddlers, and French Legionnaires. He uses case material in this essay as he did in its analytical precursor, "Ritual and Social Change." He analyzes it in terms of the presence in one field of "a multiplicity of conceptual structures" (1973b:10). Geertz alludes to alternatives for action available to each actor in the conflict, but he does not take these alternative courses of action as problematic or as relevant to the interpretation of the case. Rather, he pursues the point that to understand the conflict is to view it in terms of the ideas (concepts, beliefs, values) held by each actor and how these are different for each of them. The procedure is to identify the multiple structures that make sense of the action, each actor's behavior intelligible in terms of his own framework but confusing in terms of the others'. The emphasis is on the frameworks and not on the individual's manipulations of them. In this sense, the theoretical thrust of symbolic ethnography is similar to that of structural accounts: the focus is on the rules in terms of which individuals act (confusedly or otherwise) and not on the actors or their actions.

Symbolic ethnographers also take the position that it is possible to understand a society through an analysis of cultural performances or "representative anecdotes" (or what may also be described as "cases") that take place within it. The metaphor sometimes used to represent this procedure is that of looking through a "window." That is, the ethnographer apprehends a culture through the window of a cultural performance or "representative anecdote" and, accordingly, uses it to convey the culture to the reader. This assumption is evident in the title of the monograph, *Sherpas Through Their Rituals.* Ortner, like Geertz, posits that it is possible to understand the "inner nature" of a society by uncovering the meanings of its constituent parts. In Ortner's ethnography, as in other structural and symbolic studies, the nature of the social system is posited hypothetically and the meaning of the events within it is deduced from that hypothesized model.

The interpretation of the meaning of rituals that is supposed to lead to a discovery of the wider world in fact follows from an assumption (or set of beliefs) about that wider world. Ortner states that the "symbols of the rituals . . . lead us toward discovery of structural conflict, contradiction, and stress in the wider social and cultural world" (1978:3). This phrasing makes it seem as if an event, a cultural performance, or a text "speaks" for itself or that its meaning is or could be deduced from the event itself. However, it is clear that the meaning of an event is derived from placing it in some context, a context that is constructed by the ethnographer. Geertz acknowledges this point in his interpretation of the sheep raid in "Thick Description" when he states (1973b:28) that the "confusion of tongues model . . . is not an idea I got from [that] story . . . [rather it] is one, instructed by colleagues, students, and predecessors, I brought to it."

The point is also evident from comparing different accounts of the same people, society, or culture. For example, Christoph von Furer-Haimendorf's *The Sherpas of Nepal* (1964), which Ortner cites for ethnographic data, contains material that contradicts Ortner's interpretation of Sherpa society (cf. Samuel's 1980 review of Ortner's monograph for a comment on the discrepancy between the two accounts). He, like Ortner, found Sherpas to be generous, hospitable, friendly, and good-humored, noting "the spirit of amiability so striking in Sherpa social relations" (1964:xviii). He also found that Sherpa villages are solidary units, the boundaries of which are themselves marked by rituals. In addition, Furer-Haimendorf's description suggests that

Sherpa villages are not politically amorphous, as Ortner claims, but rather that behavior in them is regulated by village guardians who oversee compliance with rules about resource management and can sanction those who break them. Furer-Haimendorf does state that Sherpa families are self-reliant and independent units, but attributes this characteristic to a particular settlement pattern and a system of seasonal transhumance, adaptive in the Sherpas' environment, which requires geographical mobility and self-sufficiency of such families rather than to mystical "forces of anarchy." Thus, even where Ortner and Furer-Haimendorf are in agreement about certain observed facts (that is, the self-reliance of families), they are not in agreement in their explanations or interpretations of them.

(It is not only Furer-Haimendorf who disagrees with Ortner's interpretations. For example, Ortner sees the plight of the elderly as a consequence of the customary emphasis on the nuclear family. Goldstein and Beall [1981], however, offer another interpretation. To the extent that there is such a problem, they attribute it to the "impact . . . of new economic opportunities and the associated out-migration . . . " [1981:52].)

The differences between the interpretations of Ortner and Furer-Haimendorf follow from their analytical assumptions. He sees independent nuclear families and a system of social relations integrating them. For him, social order is not problematic and therefore he does not interpret Sherpa rituals as providing solutions to the problem of disorder. Ortner posits a hypothetical potential for disorder and discovers a means for managing it. She sees rituals serving that purpose. Her interpretation of the psychological function of rituals is not based upon data about actual social relations, but follows logically from her assumptions. And these assumptions are not consistent with the available data. Thus, the interpretation of Sherpa rituals follows from her view of Sherpa society. Ortner's argument is internally consistent, but it does not accord with the actualities of Sherpa life.

The interpretation of a case or a cultural performance depends upon the interpretation of society, but the interpretation of society, taken as context, itself determines the meaning attributed to the behavioral event. Ortner sees in Sherpa rituals a meaning she was bound to discover, given her assumptions about Sherpa society. With a different view of that society, as in Furer-Haimendorf's work, a different meaning is attributed to its rituals. The meaning of a case (or of a concept) is understood within its context, but since that context is not given in reality but is itself the product of analysis, the ways in which the context is bounded determines the meaning of the case (or concept). It is important for the reader to remember that contexts are constructed differently in different types of ethnographies.

Chapter 6

CONCLUSIONS

In analyzing different examples of ethnography in the preceding chap-ters, I have focused on reasoning as a standard of evaluation. By reasoning, I mean both the "activity of presenting the reasons in support of a claim, so as to show how those reasons succeed in giving strength to the claim" and the activity of constructing an argument or a "train of reasoning" which is "the sequence of interlinked claims and reasons that, between them, establish the content and force of the position being argued" (Toulmin 1979:13). Although this analytical framework is commonly used in assessing argu-ments, it is especially important to consider its role in reading ethnography because of the attention currently being paid to issues of rhetoric and reflex-ivity in discussions of ethnographic writing. To put this claims and evidence approach into context, I compare it to these other perspectives as they are represented in recent works.

RHETORIC

Within the last several years, a number of books and articles have addressed the question of the rhetoric of ethnography (Marcus and Cushman 1982, Clifford 1983, Clifford and Marcus 1986, Geertz 1988, Van Maanen

1988). These works hold that ethnography can be understood by examining the ways in which the language and organization of a text are used to persuade readers of the credibility of its claims. Geertz (1988:2–4), for example, analyzes ethnography's "rhetorical machinery" and "narrative strategies," the ways in which "knowledge claims" are advanced by "imagery, metaphor, phraseology, or voice," to counter the "view that ethnographic texts convince, insofar as they do convince, through the sheer power of their factual substantiality." The heart of his argument, similar to that of others who advocate experimental ethnography, is that "the way of saying is the what of saying" (1988:68).

There seems to be little question that analyzing the rhetoric of an ethnography contributes to an appreciation of it. It seems equally clear that this approach to reading ethnography complements that of examining its reasoning (cf. Marcus and Cushman 1982:56). A reader should be alert not only to questions of evidence and to textual organization in an ethnography such as The Nuer, but also to its rhetorical features (cf. Clifford 1983:126–27, 137, Rosaldo 1986:87–96, Geertz 1988:49–72). However, it is also important to note ways in which the two approaches differ. For example, the analytical categories applied in the rhetoric of ethnography are those of literary criticism (cf. Marcus and Cushman 1982, Spiro 1986, Clifford 1986, Marcus 1986, Roth 1989), not those of reasoning. A rhetorical analysis concerns the effects of narrative voice; that of reasoning concerns the relationships between claims and evidence. The two approaches can lead to different assessments of the authenticity of the same ethnographic writing.

The issue of textual organization is one example of such a difference. Although the narrative structure of traditional ethnographies, containing chapters on "geography, kinship, economics, politics, and religion," may simply reflect the theoretical view that societies are divided (or divisible) into such analytical "units" (Marcus and Cushman 1982:31), it would appear that it is more than that. Rather, the particular order in which these units are presented may also be seen as a train of reasoning. That is, to begin an account by examining a people's geography not only identifies where they are located in space, but also addresses questions of the ecological or material conditions facilitating and limiting their way of life. Similarly, chapters on kinship, economics, and politics focus on the ways in which people maintain themselves biologically and socially and adapt to their natural and social environments. Ending an ethnography with a chapter on religion also makes sense, if it is assumed that religion (as a cultural system) formulates a people's view of the way their world is and ought to be that ultimately determines the organization of their society. In short, the format of such ethnographies constitutes steps in an argument about how a society is organized and what explains the behavior of its people. It seems little different in principle from that found in an ethnography such as Sherpas Through Their Ritu-

als, in which the ethnographer moves from the "surface contours" of a society to the "inner connections and interactions" that hold it together.

Another example is that of generalization. Advocates of experimental ethnography note that traditional ethnographies contain statements about the people being described, as though the description applies to all of the people in question, without reference to the actions and experiences of particular individuals or to differences among them. Marcus and Cushman refer to this sort of practice as an account of "common denominator people" (Marcus and Cushman 1982:32; cf. Rosaldo 1986:94), contending that it is a rhetorical device used to establish the legitimacy of anthropology as a scientific discipline. However, it is important to recognize that the issue is not merely one of rhetoric. It is also a matter of analytical focus: the language of an ethnographic text is related to the level(s) of analysis being undertaken. Thus, any ethnography that takes the system as the unit of analysis and description (cf. Marcus and Cushman 1982:32, Ortner 1984:151–52) will more than likely contain such statements, and, in so far as they refer to modes of thought, it may not be inappropriate to do so. (It would be inappropriate when a society or culture is complex or heterogeneous, that is, when there are segments of the population who have different ways of looking at or thinking about things, as is usually the case.) On the other hand, ethnographies that focus on modes of action more than likely contain data about individuals and the ways in which they behave in the face of various opportunities and alternative courses of action available to them. That is, the locus of description (system or individual) is related to the level of analysis (modes of thought or modes of action), and it is therefore appropriate when reading ethnography to identify what is being described before assessing the terms in which it is being described.

The authority of ethnographic texts is another topic of central importance in the literature on the rhetoric of ethnography (cf. Marcus and Cushman 1982, Clifford 1983, Geertz 1988). There it is commonly held that the ethnographer's presence in the field is the basis for establishing the credibility of an ethnographic account. For example, Geertz asserts (without presenting evidence of who takes what seriously) that

> The ability of anthropologists to get us to take what they say seriously has less to do with either a factual look or an air of conceptual elegance than it has with their capacity to convince us that what they say is a result of their having actually penetrated (or, if you prefer, been penetrated by) another form of life, of having, one way or another, truly "been there" (1988:4–5).

From this rhetorical perspective, the crucial evidence in an ethnography is that which attests to the ethnographer's having been in the field. This evidence includes, among other things, indications in the ethnographic text of the conditions and experiences of fieldwork and the presentation of photographs, maps, and drawings (Marcus and Cushman 1982:33, Clifford 1983: 118, Geertz 1988:66–68). As Clifford puts it (1983:118), because the photographs included within an ethnography assert the presence of the ethnographer among the people being described, they signal ethnographic authority.

From a claims and evidence point of view, there are two major problems with this rhetorical position. First, although these visual data can serve as evidence for an ethnographer's claims about the existence of the things represented, they do not necessarily indicate the presence of the ethnographer in the field. That is, photos are not necessarily proof of the anthropologist's having done fieldwork or of having really been there. For example, of the forty-one photographs in *The Nuer*, thirteen were taken by people other than Evans-Pritchard and of the nine photographs in *Kinship and Marriage Among the Nuer*, two were taken by a colonial administrator—including one, "A maiden, smoking pipe," that Geertz (1988:66) cites as an indication of Evans-Pritchard's having been in the field. Furthermore, as Johnson (1979:165) notes, Evans-Pritchard uses in *The Nuer* a photograph (Plate IX, facing page 72), entitled "Harpoon-fishing from canoe (Sobat river)," that not only was taken by someone other than the ethnographer but that depicts men who are in all likelihood Shilluk, not Nuer. Ironically, that same photo, as Johnson remarks, also appears on the cover of the paperback editions of the book.

The other difficulty is more fundamental. It is that the ethnographer's presence in the field is not evidence for the claims he or she makes about the people, society, or culture in question. Indeed, those writing about the authority of ethnography either do not address the issue of evidence in these terms or else fail to give full measure to it. Rather, they assume " . . . that ethnography is a process of interpretation, not of explanation" and choose not to discuss "modes of authority based on natural-scientific epistemologies" (Clifford 1983:142). The criteria of reasoning used to assess the authenticity of ethnography are dismissed in studies of its rhetoric.

REFLEXIVITY

The issue of reflexivity, the ethnographer's recounting of and reflection upon his or her experience, is another concern of experimental writing, closely related to that of rhetoric and ethnographic authority. Reflexive ethnographies represent, as Geertz puts it, an "I-witnessing approach to the construction of cultural descriptions" (1988:78), bringing together "fieldwork as personal encounter and ethnography as reliable account" (1988:84). Just as textual indication of the anthropologist's *presence* in the field is taken as a basis for accepting an ethnography's claims, detailing the ethnographer's *experience* is seen as crucial for establishing the validity of his or her interpretation. A central assumption underlying this sort of ethnographic writing, as Roth notes, is that "[s]elf-conscious self-representation signals a reliable narrator and confers credibility on the text" (1989:557). A serious limitation of reflexive ethnography, however, is that it confuses the process of discovery with that of verification.

This is not to say that reflexivity is an unimportant issue. Detailing the ways in which data are constructed and/or discovered, especially as a product of the interaction between ethnographer and the people with whom he or she is concerned, can enable the reader to assess those data and therefore the arguments based upon them. This rationale, of course, is not peculiar to reflexive ethnography. The practice of describing research procedures—explicating analytical categories and specifying the operations by which data are measured—characterizes standard ethnographies (in which such information is typically contained either in an introductory chapter or in an appendix) as well as arguments produced in other empirical disciplines. However, an account of the ethnographer's experience—what happened to the anthropologist—does not provide evidence for assessing his or her claims about the people, the society, or the culture among whom or within which fieldwork was done. Rather, assertions contained in a reflexive account about the people being depicted often make sense only in reference to or in the context of the author/ethnographer's more conventional ethnography.

In Rabinow's *Reflections on Fieldwork in Morocco* (1977), for example, the point of the narrative is clear. "This book," he states, "is an account of my experiences in Morocco. . . . [It] is a reconstruction of a set of encounters that occurred while doing fieldwork. . . . a studied condensation of a swirl of people, places, and feelings" (1977:4, 6). Rabinow introduces individuals he got to know in the course of his fieldwork: a hotel owner, a tutor of Arabic, a curer, a shopkeeper/pimp, a prostitute, an informant, and a young man who became his friend. (The order in which these characters are introduced appears to parallel Rabinow's progression into fieldwork as well as his comprehension of Moroccan culture, moving from French colonial to Moroccan native, from city to country, from surface contours to inner connections.) He describes various episodes in which he engages with them (for example, a wedding, a curing ceremony, a country excursion, a sexual encounter), and he recalls feelings he had when interacting with them (resentment, anger, frustration, excitement, bewilderment, happiness). The account is descriptive, representing his fieldwork experiences as they more or less happened; it details, in part, how the ethnographer acquired some of his data. Yet, despite Rabinow's contention, this process of discovery is not directly connected to the interpretations about Moroccan culture and society that he incorporates into his account. Rather, his claims in this regard are based upon other data. Rabinow's reflections upon his personal experiences may be interesting, but they do not constitute grounds for his conclusions about Moroccan ways of evaluating the world and their relationships in and to it. His experiences, and his analysis of them, are unrelated to his interpretation, except as rhetorical devices.

Take, for example, Rabinow's analyses of Moroccan values which are interspersed throughout the monograph. He uses anecdotes about particular encounters to illustrate wider cultural themes, much as Geertz deploys his attendance at a particular cockfight to anchor a discussion of Balinese sensibility. Rabinow's interpretations of aspects of Moroccan culture (1977:48-69)—generosity and independence, religious brotherhoods and curing power, social status and sexual behavior, and the standards in terms of which all of these are judged—depend on his explication of native concepts (*karim, baraka, moqaddem, wlad siyyed, dikr, shih, 'ayyan, shal, bezzef*). Rabinow's representations of Moroccan culture do not depend on his reflections on his fieldwork experience, but on his analysis of data conventionally contained in standard ethnography (especially in the modes of thought type). Indeed, Rabinow alludes in a footnote (1977:7) to a previous work, *Symbolic Domination: Cultural Form and Historical Change in Morocco* (1975), that constitutes a "complementary and more traditionally anthropological treatment of the data covered here [in *Reflections*]." Without his having done his analysis in the other ethnography, it would seem that Rabinow's understanding of Moroccan culture as presented in *Reflections* would not be as intelligible as it is, either to him or to his readers.

Favret-Saada's *Deadly Words: Witchcraft in the Bocage* (1980 [1977]) raises a different issue about reflexive ethnography. The monograph concerns the ways in which people in the countryside of western France explain misfortune. They believe, according to the ethnographer, that a "witch" speaks words that can cause affliction to someone who is thus said to be "bewitched" and that the "bewitched" can be cured through the services of an "unwitcher," who "takes on himself . . . words originally spoken to his client, and turns them back on to their initial sender . . . [becoming] a screen between sender and receiver" (1980:9). Witchcraft is thus a type of discourse in which people attribute to words the power to harm and to counter harm.

Although this thesis may not be unusual in the ethnographic literature on witchcraft, what sets Favret-Saada's study apart is its detailing of the ways in which the ethnographer acquired her data. The ethnographer argues that since the peasants of the Bocage believe that words are powerful, they speak

them, and about them, only when attempting to exercise that power. Therefore, Favret-Saada claims, she could obtain information about these beliefs
only by taking part in the discourse itself. As she states: " . . . *the discourse of
witchcraft is such that to gain access to it one must be in a position to sustain it
oneself*" (1980:22). Accordingly, when put in this position by informants,
she permitted them to take her for an "unwitcher" and became herself the
client of one. In *Reflections*, Rabinow's interpretation of Moroccan culture is
not contingent upon the fieldwork experiences he describes or upon the
reader's knowledge of them. By contrast, Favret-Saada argues that without
her participation in the lives of her informants there would be no data to
analyze. She had to become a participant in order to become an observer.
Therefore, Favret-Saada recounts her experiences because they constitute in
large part the descriptive material of her ethnography.

    If the circumstances of the context of discovery differentiate *Deadly
Words* as a reflexive account, the kinds of data it contains are essentially no
different from those recorded in other modes of thought ethnographies. In
depicting the belief system of the people with whom she interacted, Favret-
Saada introduces and explicates native concepts (such as '*unwitcher*,' having
'*weak*' or '*strong blood*,' being '*caught*,' and the '*force*' of witches and
unwitches), as well as native discourse. This discourse is presented in terms
of several examples of misfortune, including the dialogue about them that
occurred between ethnographer and informants. (Although cultural concepts and native statements have been translated in the English edition of
the ethnography, they are italicized, as is customary when presenting such
data, and set in single quotation marks.)

    Favret-Saada notes her focus on such verbal behavior by contrasting it
with what is emphasized in other ethnographic accounts of witchcraft. In
those studies, she suggests, "the sociological context of witchcraft matters and
especially of the particular positions of the opponents in the local struggles
for prestige and power . . . usually constitute the subject-matter . . . " (1980:21).
She repeatedly indicates her plans to address these topics in a "forthcoming
volume," in which she will analyze, for example, "unwitching seances" (p.18,
n. 8; cf. pp. 160, 185), "the relative autonomy of the discourse of witchcraft in
relation to the sociological determinants usually proposed to account for its
use" (p.21, n. 13), and the "interaction" between witch and bewitched (p.
113, n. 6). It appears that such subsequent interpretations will be less concerned with the discovery process and more so with substantive issues.
Indeed, this other account promises to take Favret-Saada beyond the "mid-
way speculations" of her current ethnography, thereby constituting a basis for
more fully appraising its claims about witchcraft in the Bocage.

    Favret-Saada's allusions to a forthcoming study suggest an important
similarity between reflexive ethnographies such as *Deadly Words* and Rabi-

now's *Reflections on Fieldwork*. Both refer to companion accounts in which there is less concern about the fieldwork experiences of the ethnographer and more about the culture in which the research was done. In Rabinow's case, the standard account was published prior to the reflexive one; in Favret-Saada's case, the order is reversed: the reflexive account is to be followed a more conventional anthropological analysis.

In other anthropological works, still another reason is given for describing the ethnographer's experience. In this case, it is introduced not because it is a device for presenting data (as in *Reflections*) nor because it was necessary for generating data (as in *Deadly Words*), but because it is supposed to be essential for understanding data. In this sort of reflexive ethnography, it is assumed, as Roth points out, that the "sensitivity of the investigator serve[s] as a litmus test for the authenticity of the account" (1989:557). Yet, there are two difficulties with this kind of ethnography: documenting the experience of others, and establishing the relevance of the ethnographer's experience for the interpretation of the experience of others. Both are matters of verification.

Rosaldo's "Grief and the Headhunter's Rage" (1988 [1984]) is an example of this sort of reflexive ethnography and its problems. In this essay, Rosaldo revises his interpretation of why the Ilongot of the Philippines, among whom he had done fieldwork, engage in headhunting. An older Ilongot man would claim, Rosaldo asserts, that he headhunts because "rage, born of grief, impels him to kill his fellow human beings . . . [thereby enabling him] to vent and hopefully throw away the anger of his bereavement," (1988:178). Rosaldo acknowledges that he did not understand that statement "for the longest time," adding that, "It was not until I was repositioned through lived experience that I became better able to grasp that Ilongot older men mean precisely what they say when they describe the anger in bereavement as the source of their desire to cut off human heads" (1988:178–79). That is, it was not until he experienced his own grief and rage, precipitated by the accidental death of his wife (and co-worker), that he began to understand Ilongot explanations of their behavior.

There are several issues to be considered in assessing Rosaldo's argument. One concerns his failure to mention Ilongot women, leaving the reader to wonder whether their experiences are different from those of men, and, if so, how should they interpreted. Another concerns the scope of his claims, since clearly he himself, on becoming bereaved and enraged, did not act out or upon his feelings by taking a head. However, in the context of examining the credibility of the claims he does make, a more pertinent question focuses on the grounds for his conclusions about the emotional states of Ilongot men. What data does he provide in support of his contentions about their feelings? He refers to their statements about grief and rage (1988:178, 179), yet points out that these may well express a "cultural stereotype," how they ought to feel rather than how they actually feel (cf. 1988:191). Moreover, he does not present verbal evidence such as native terms, translated or otherwise, for such feelings. The absence of such linguistic materials is particularly noteworthy, since Rosaldo cites another ethnographic account (about the feelings of Nyakyusa) in which the ethnographer (Godfrey Wilson) does present them (cf. 1988:188). Furthermore, Rosaldo acknowledges that the "rage of older men . . . [is] without elaboration in speech, song, or ritual" (1988:192). Even if the Ilongot did so symbolize their sentiments, interpreting them would still be problematic. As Rosaldo notes, one "can assume neither that individuals do nor do not feel the sentiments they express during a funeral" or in other rituals of mourning (1988:187). In short, the ethnographer's attributions about Ilongot feelings are based on scant evidence and the meaning of that which is presented is ambiguous.

In addition to problems of substantiating such attributions, there remain questions about the relevance of Rosaldo's experience to his explanation of the Ilongot. Models of the grieving process raise doubts about Rosaldo's interpretation. For example, in Bowlby's analysis of bereavement (1980), people respond to such loss in a sequence of phases or stages, each marked by different cognitive and emotional characteristics. These stages include those of denial, searching and yearning, disorganization, and reorganization. The first is associated with a feeling of numbness, the second with anger or rage, the third with despair and depression, and the last with improved functioning and a renewal of the capacity for experiencing gratification. What is important about this model is that rage is typically an acute feeling, severe but of short duration, and characteristic of an early stage of response to loss.

In these terms, Rosaldo's account of Ilongot grief, rage, and headhunting does not make sense. Rosaldo describes three elements that he sees as underlying headhunting raids. Reversing the order in which he discusses them, they are: the "acute agonies" of older men who are supposed to headhunt after experiencing "rage born of devastating loss" (1988:191), the "chronic adolescent turmoil" of Ilongot "young men coming of age" who "desire nothing so much as to take a head" (1988:191), and the suitability of "historical conditions" that constrain or facilitate the activity of raiding (1988:190). The first appears to fit the model, since it is older men who, in a state of rage, initiate headhunting ("set the processes of headhunting in motion") (1988:191), although Rosaldo does not mention anything about the timing of raids in relation to the onset of bereavement which would link the emotional upheaval of the early stage of grieving to the act that it is supposed to motivate. The case of young men, however, does not fit the model (nor is it consistent with the rest of Rosaldo's analysis), since they are neither in an acute emotional state nor responding to a loss. Finally, the undertaking of raids in conjunction with "historical contingencies" seems not to reflect the intense emotional state of rage, understood as a spontaneous, uncontrollable, and grief-stricken reaction, but rather a calculated plan for acquiring the status of manhood and/or for exercising leadership (cf.1988:181).

⌈In short, introducing the experience of the ethnographer into an account does not necessarily shed light on the experiences of others. This is especially so if the applicability of that experience, however it may reposition and sensitize the researcher, is not carefully considered. Recounting an ethnographer's experience is not an adequate substitute for a reasoned analysis of the feelings and actions of his or her informants.⌋

READING ETHNOGRAPHY

The "thorny problems of verification" (Clifford 1986:25) evident in the "literary treatment of ethnography" (Marcus 1986:263) and in the "self-consciousness or self-absorption" of reflexive ethnography (Clifford 1986:15; cf. Rosaldo 1988:182) make it imperative to evaluate anthropologists' accounts of human behavior and social life from the perspective of the ways in which they validate their interpretations and construct their arguments. ⌊These tasks require the reader of an ethnography, as indicated in preceding chapters, to examine the relationships between its claims and data as well as the ways in which its questions, answers, and evidence are arranged. There is no shortcut for doing the hard work of analyzing ethnographic argumentation, but there are some guidelines that may be of help in this endeavor.⌋

The title of an ethnography, for example, provides one way of discerning its argument. Perhaps you cannot tell a book by its cover, but paying attention to the title may afford a first clue to what it is about. Although *The Nuer* may not be particularly informative, its subtitle, *A Description of the Modes of Livelihood and Political Institutions of a Nilotic People,* further delineates the area of inquiry, indicating both which topics are included and which are excluded. That is, it is not about kinship and marriage or religion. Likewise, *Political Leadership among Swat Pathans* suggests its theme is the activity of individuals, thereby indicating a contrast with Evans-Pritchard's focus on the constitutive rules of a system. Moreover, the title of Leach's monograph, *Political Systems of Highland Burma: A Study of Kachin Social Structure,* signals its central problem: the relationship between plural systems and a singular structure. Correspondingly, Bailey's *Tribe, Caste, and Nation: A Study of Political Activity and Political Change in Highland Orissa* suggests similarities and differences between his ethnography and these others: it too deals with multiple systems, although it would appear to focus on individuals, insofar as they are implied as agents engaged in activity. Of course, without examining these ethnographies in detail, a reader cannot expect to be able to grasp the arguments they contain, but a glance at their titles can provide a guideline to them.

Similarly, some insight as to the nature of an ethnography's argument can be derived from study of its textual organization as reflected in its table of contents. For example, the chapters of *The Nuer* move from the goals that people pursue to the rules that regulate that pursuit. In *Political Systems of Highland Burma*, the train of reasoning is presented in three parts: a statement of the "problem" (the apparently confusing distribution of different types of people on the ground), a description of the concepts (the "structural categories") in terms of which people classify and organize their relationships, and an analysis of the ways in which they manipulate their concepts and their relationships ("structural variability"). In Barth's monograph, the steps are from various kinds of constraints on people's actions and relationships through the nature of political relationships to an account of relationships between leaders and their followers and finally of those between leaders. The parts of *Tribe, Caste, and Nation* address in sequence the different "structures" identified in the title followed by an analysis of political activity (manifest in the case of a dispute) in which individuals act in accord with one or more of these structures. And Ortner organizes the chapters of her account of the Sherpas to advance her interpretation from a statement of the problem ("What keeps things in order?") to an analysis of "rituals" as the means of conflict resolution within the family, between families, and within the community at large. An ethnography's argument, as outlined in its table of contents, may well seem more evident after a close reading of the book, but looking at it carefully beforehand can serve to orient the reader's attention to it.

An ethnography's index can also be a source of information for identifying its argument. For example, in the index of *The Nuer* the reader finds several entries regarding feuds and hostilities as well as the means of settling them. These items suggest the ethnographer's analytical problem: the causes and the nature of conflict in a society in which an expected means of resolving it is not present. Similarly, in *Sherpas Through Their Rituals*, the reader finds five separate references to the problematic nature of "social order." The characterization and repetition of this term should alert readers to its import for the argument of the ethnography.

Moreover, the listing of vernacular terms in an ethnography's index can provide clues to what it takes as problematic and to its level of analysis. For example, in the index of *The Nuer* there are over fifty such terms and in that of *Sherpas Through Their Rituals* some forty native terms are listed. Even organizational ethnographies, focusing on modes of action, include vernacular terms in their indices, although typically many fewer. For example, Barth lists six terms, all relating to the system of land tenure which is basic to Swat Pathan political leadership.

Considering the hard work that reading ethnography entails, it is important to recall, by way of a few concluding remarks, the reasons for undertaking it. First of all, it enables the reader to grasp what any particular essay or monograph is about. It is not only that ethnographies often appear to be simply descriptive; more importantly, their analytical problems and interpretive conclusions are typically embedded in, and implied by, the descriptive materials (that is, the ethnographic facts) they contain and the order in which they are presented. So, sorting out what are propositions and what are data for them, determining whether or not claims and evidence warrant each other, and uncovering the structure of an ethnography facilitates an evaluation of it. Moreover, the hope is that such effort, of critically assessing ethnographies and of distinguishing between weak arguments and strong ones, will produce better fieldwork and will lead to the writing of better ethnographies and to the advancement of the theories that inform them.

⌊Reading ethnography in this way can also provide a means of classifying theoretical frameworks and presuppositions.⌡Not in the sense of delineating substantive topics (that is, particular hypotheses and findings in the subfields of social anthropology), but in the sense of depicting key approaches to them as reflected in an emphasis on either modes of thought or modes of action. This is not to say that dividing ethnographies into these two broad categories is the only way in which they may be classified or that all ethnographies can be easily fit into them. However, it seems that this is a useful distinction, since they appear to be basic categories of analysis and description, others being variations or amalgams of them. That is, this classification provides a model for analyzing the nature of anthropological argumentation. It should be noted, however,⌈that reading ethnography reveals the way in which arguments are cast: it tells the reader what kinds of questions the ethnographer is addressing and the kinds of data relevant to them. It does not necessarily reveal the questions that shaped the ethnographer's fieldwork, only those that shape the analysis and interpretation of its results.⌉

Reading an ethnography contributes not only to understanding the particular society or culture it represents, but also, through comparative scholarship, to knowledge about societies and cultures in general. That is, typically what anthropologists compare are not the ethnographic facts of different societies or culture, but the models that they construct for making sense of them. For example, descriptively, *The Nuer* is about the political system of a cattle-keeping people in East Africa and *Sherpas Through Their Rituals* is about religion in a Buddhist culture in Nepal. But on an analytical level, both accounts are about how social order is maintained in the face of conditions that theoretically undermine it. In each case the particular con-ditions differ (a bellicose, transient people living in a society without cen-tralized authority and a people living in a society without secular controls whose religion fosters antisocial tendencies) and the solutions differ (a seg-mentary system and redeeming rituals), but analytically they are compara-ble, and comparing them can lead to a better understanding of the common practices and processes underlying diverse ethnographic cases.

This, of course, is what makes reading ethnography the essential activ-ity that it is. The fundamental goal of social anthropology, it has been said, is to understand human behavior and social life. Since ethnographies are the main product of anthropological inquiry, they constitute the bases for anthropological knowledge. Therefore, a most important reason for reading ethnography is to grasp not only what ethnographers do, but why they do it. In this respect, we would do well to remember Geertz's dictum, with which this book begins: anthropologists (or at least social anthropologists) do ethnography, and therefore to understand ethnography is to begin to com-prehend what (social) anthropology as a field is about. Thus, reading ethnography is central to the wider anthropological enterprise of which it is part.

Adler, Mortimer J.
  1940   *How to Read a Book*. New York: Simon and Schuster.

Bailey, F. G.
  1960   *Tribe, Caste, and Nation*. Manchester: Manchester University Press.
  1969   *Strategems and Spoils*. New York: Schocken Books.

Barnes, John A.
  1971   *Three Styles in the Study of Kinship*. London: Tavistock Publications.

Barth, Fredrik.
  1959   *Political Leadership Among Swat Pathans*. London: The Athlone Press.

Basso, Keith H., and Henry A. Selby, eds.
  1976   *Meaning in Anthropology*. Albuquerque: University of New Mexico Press.

Bateson, Gregory.
  1958   *Naven*. Stanford: Stanford University Press.

Beidelman, T. O.
  1970   Nuer Priests and Prophets: Charisma, Authority, and Power Among the Nuer. In *The Translation of Culture*, edited by T. O. Beidelman, 375–415. London: Tavistock Publications.

Boissevain, Jeremy.
  1985   Ethnographic Fieldwork. In *The Social Science Encyclopedia*, edited by Adam Kuper and Jessica Kuper, 272–74. London: Routledge and Kegan Paul.

Bowlby, John.
  1980   *Attachment and Loss, Vol.3: Loss, Sadness, and Depression*. New York: Basic Books.

Clifford, James.
  1983   On Ethnographic Authority. *Representations* 1:2:118–46.
  1986   Introduction: Partial Truths. In *Writing Culture: The Poetics and Politics of Ethnography*, edited by James Clifford and George Marcus, 1–26. Berkeley: University of California Press.
  1988   *The Predicament of Culture: Twentieth Century Ethnography, Literature, and Art.* Cambridge: Harvard University Press.

Clifford, James, and George E. Marcus, eds.
  1986   *Writing Culture: The Poetics and Politics of Ethnography.* Berkeley: University of California Press.

Cohen, Abner.
  1969   *Custom and Politics in Urban Africa.* Berkeley: University of California Press.
  1974   *Two Dimensional Man.* Berkeley: University of California Press.

Connor, Linda.
  1984   Comments. *Current Anthropology* 25:3:271.

Crapanzano, Vincent.
  1986   Hermes' Dilemma: The Masking of Subversion in Ethnographic Description. In *Writing Culture*, edited by James Clifford and George E. Marcus, 51–76. Berkeley: University of California Press.

Crick, Malcom.
  1976   *Explorations in Language and Meaning.* New York: John Wiley and Sons.

D'Andrade, Roy G.
  1984   Cultural Meaning Systems. In *Culture Theory: Essays on Mind, Self, and Emotion*, edited by Richard A. Shweder and Robert A. LeVine, 88–119. Cambridge: Cambridge University Press.

Dumont, Jean-Paul.
  1978   *The Headman and I.* Austin: The University of Texas Press.

Dumont, Louis.
  1975   Preface to the French edition of E. E. Evans-Pritchard's *The Nuer.* In *Studies in Social Anthropology*, edited by J. H. M. Beattie and R. G. Lienhardt, 328–42. Oxford: Oxford University Press.

Durkheim, Emile.
  1938   *The Rules of Sociological Method.* New York: The Free Press.

Edgerton, Robert B., and L. L. Langness.
  1974   *Methods and Styles in the Study of Culture.* San Francisco: Chandler and Sharp Publishers.

Evans-Pritchard, E. E.
   1937   *Witchcraft, Oracles, and Magic Among the Azande.* Oxford: The Clarendon Press.
   1940a   *The Nuer.* Oxford: The Clarendon Press.
   1940b   The Nuer of Southern Sudan. In *African Political Systems,* edited by Meyer Fortes and E. E. Evans-Pritchard, 272–96. London: Oxford University Press.
   1951a   *Kinship and Marriage Among the Nuer.* Oxford: The Clarendon Press.
   1951b   *Social Anthropology.* London: Cohen and West.
   1956   *Nuer Religion.* Oxford: The Clarendon Press.
   1962   *Essays in Social Anthropology.* London: Faber and Faber.

Favret-Saada, Jeanne.
   1980   *Deadly Words: Witchcraft in the Bocage.* Cambridge: Cambridge University Press.

Firth, Raymond.
   1936   *We, the Tikopia.* London: Allen and Unwin.
   1951   *Elements of Social Organization.* Boston: Beacon Press.
   1954   Social Organization and Social Change. *Journal of the Royal Anthropological Institute* 84:1–20.
   1955   Some Principles of Social Organization. *Journal of the Royal Anthropological Institute* 85:1–18.
   1964a   *Essays on Social Organization and Values.* London: The Athlone Press.
   1964b   Social Organization and Social Change. In *Essays on Social Organization and Values,* 30–58. London: The Athlone Press.
   1964c   Some Principles of Social Organization. In *Essays on Social Organization and Values,* 59–87. London: The Athlone Press.
   1975   An Appraisal of Modern Social Anthropology. *Annual Review of Anthropology* 4:1–25.
   1985   Degrees of Intelligibility. In *Reason and Morality,* edited by Joanna Overing, 29–46. London: Tavistock Publications.

Fortes, M., and E. E. Evans-Pritchard, eds.
   1940   *African Political Systems.* London: Oxford University Press.

Fortes, Meyer.
   1945   *The Dynamics of Clanship Among the Tallensi.* London: Oxford University Press.
   1949   *The Web of Kinship Among the Tallensi.* London: Oxford University Press.
   1970a   *Time and Social Structure and Other Essays.* New York: Humanities Press.
   1970b   Analysis and Description in Social Anthropology. In *Time and Social Structure and Other Essays,* 127–46. New York: Humanities Press.
   1970c   Time and Social Structure: An Ashanti Case Study. In *Time and Social Structure and Other Essays,* 1–32. New York: Humanities Press.

1978   An Anthropologist's Apprenticeship. *Annual Review of Anthropology* 7:1–30.

Geertz, Clifford.
1973a   *The Interpretation of Cultures*. New York: Basic Books.
1973b   Thick Description: Toward an Interpretive Theory of Culture. In *The Interpretation of Cultures*. 3–30. New York: Basic Books.
1973c   Religion as a Cultural System. In *The Interpretation of Cultures*, 87–125. New York: Basic Books.
1973d   Deep Play: Notes on the Balinese Cockfight. In *The Interpretation of Cultures*, 412–53. New York: Basic Books.
1973e   Ritual and Social Change: A Javanese Example. In *The Interpretation of Cultures*, 142–69. New York: Basic Books.
1976   "From the Native's Point of View": On the Nature of Anthropological Understanding. In *Meaning in Anthropology*, edited by Keith H. Basso and Henry A. Selby, 221–37. Albuquerque: University of New Mexico Press.
1988   *Works and Lives: The Anthropologist as Author*. Stanford: Stanford University Press.

Gellner, Ernest.
1970   Concepts and Society. In *Rationality*, edited by Bryan Wilson, 18–49. Oxford: Basil Blackwell.

Gluckman, Max.
1940   Analysis of a Social Situation in Modern Zululand. *Bantu Studies* 14:1:1–30; 14:2:147–74.
1956   *Custom and Conflict in Africa*. Oxford: Basil Blackwell.
1961   Ethnographic Data in British Social Anthropology. *The Sociological Review* 9:1:5–17.

Goldstein, Melvyn C., and Cynthia M. Beall.
1981   Modernization and Aging in the Third and Fourth World: Views from the Rural Hinterland of Nepal. *Human Organization* 40:1:48–55.

Goodenough, Ward.
1970   *Description and Comparison in Cultural Anthropology*. Chicago: Aldine Publishing Company.

Gough, Kathleen.
1971   Nuer Kinship: A Re-examination. In *The Translation of Culture*, edited by T. O. Beidelman, 79–121. London: Tavistock Publications.

Holy, Ladislav.
1979   The Segmentary Lineage Structure and Its Existential Status. In *Segmentary Lineage Systems Reconsidered* (The Queen's University Papers in Social Anthropology, volume 4), edited by Ladislav Holy, 1–22. Belfast: Department of Social Anthropology, The Queen's University of Belfast.

Holy, Ladislav, and Milan Stuchlik.
    1983   *Actions, Norms, and Representations*. Cambridge: Cambridge University Press.

Johnson, Douglas H.
    1979   Nuer or Shilluk? *Man* (n.s.) 14:1:165.
    1981   The Fighting Nuer: Primary Sources and the Origins of a Stereotype. *Africa* 51:508–27.

Kaberry, Phyllis.
    1957   Malinowski's Contribution to Field-work Methods and the Writing of Ethnography. In *Man and Culture*, edited by Raymond Firth, 71–91. London: Routledge & Kegan Paul.

Karp, Ivan, and Kent Maynard.
    1983   Reading *The Nuer*. *Current Anthropology* 24:4:481–503.

Keesing, Roger M.
    1974   Theories of Culture. *Annual Review of Anthropology* 3:73–97.
    1987   Anthropology as Interpretive Quest. *Current Anthropology* 28:2:161–76.

Kelly, Raymond C.
    1985   *The Nuer Conquest*. Ann Arbor: The University of Michigan Press.

Leach, E. R.
    1954   *Political Systems of Highland Burma*. Boston: Beacon Press.
    1961   *Pul Eliya: A Village in Ceylon*. Cambridge: Cambridge University Press.

Liebow, Elliot.
    1967   *Tally's Corner*. Boston: Little, Brown.

Malinowski, Bronislaw.
    1922   *Argonauts of the Western Pacific*. London: Routledge and Kegan Paul.
    1926   *Crime and Custom in Savage Society*. London: Routledge and Kegan Paul.
    1935   *Coral Gardens and Their Magic*. London: Allen and Unwin.

Marcus, George E.
    1980   Rhetoric and the Ethnographic Genre in Anthropological Research. *Current Anthropology* 21:4:507–10.
    1986   Afterword: Ethnographic Writing and Anthropological Careers. In *Writing Culture: The Poetics and Politics of Ethnography*, edited by James Clifford and George E. Marcus, 262–66. Berkeley: University of California Press.

Marcus, George E., and Dick Cushman.
    1982   Ethnographies as Texts. *Annual Review of Anthropology* 11:25–69.

Meeker, Michael E.
    1989   *The Pastoral Son and the Spirit of Patriarchy: Religion, Society, and Per-*

son *Among East African Stock Keepers*. Madison: The University of
Wisconsin Press.

Mitchell, Clyde.
1956   *The Yao Village*. Manchester: Manchester University Press.

O'Neill, John, ed.
1973   *Modes of Individualism and Collectivism*. London: Heinemann.

Ortner, Sherry B.
1978   *Sherpas Through Their Rituals*. Cambridge: Cambridge University Press.
1984   Theory in Anthropology Since the Sixties. *Comparative Studies in Society and History* 26:1:126–66.

Peristiany, J. G.
1974   Introduction. In Emile Durkheim, *Sociology and Philosophy*. Translated by D. F. Pocock, vii–xxxii. New York: The Free Press.

Pitt-Rivers, Julian.
1967   Contextual Analysis and the Locus of the Model. *European Journal of Sociology* 8: 15–34.

Pocock, D. F.
1961   *Social Anthropology*. London: Sheed and Ward.

Rabinow, Paul.
1975   *Symbolic Domination: Cultural Form and Historical Change in Morocco*. Chicago: University of Chicago Press.
1977   *Reflections on Fieldwork in Morocco*. Berkeley: University of California Press.

Richards, A. I.
1941   A Problem of Anthropological Approach. *Bantu Studies* 15:45–52.

Rosaldo, Renato.
1986   From the Door of his Tent: The Fieldworker and the Inquisitor. In *Writing Culture*, edited by James Clifford and George E. Marcus, 77–97. Berkeley: The University of California Press.
1988   Grief and a Headhunter's Rage: On the Cultural Force of Emotions. In *Text, Play, and Story: The Construction and Reconstruction of Self and Society*, edited by Edward M. Bruner, 178–95. Prospect Heights, Illinois: Waveland Press.

Roseberry, William.
1982   Balinese Cockfights and the Seduction of Anthropology. *Social Research* 49:1013–28.

Roth, Paul A.
1989   Ethnography Without Tears. *Current Anthropology* 30:5:555–69.

Sahlins, Marshall D.
    1961   The Segmentary Lineage: An Organization of Predatory Expansion. *American Anthropologist* 63:332–45.

Samuel, Geoffrey.
    1980   Sherpas Through Their Rituals. *Man* (n.s.) 15:2:400–401.

Sangren, P. Steven.
    1988   Rhetoric and the Authority of Ethnography: "Postmodernism" and the Social Reproduction of Texts. *Current Anthropology* 29: 3: 405–35.

Schneider, David M.
    1968   *American Kinship: A Cultural Account.* Englewood Cliffs: Prentice-Hall.
    1976   Notes Toward a Theory of Culture. In *Meaning in Anthropology*, edited by Keith H. Basso and Henry A. Selby, 197–220. Albuquerque: University of New Mexico Press.

Searle, John.
    1969   *Speech Acts.* Cambridge: Cambridge University Press.

Shankman, Paul.
    1984   The Thick and the Thin: On the Interpretive Theoretical Program of Clifford Geertz. *Current Anthropology* 25:3261–79.

Southall, Aidan.
    1976   Nuer and Dinka are People: Ecology, Ethnicity, and Logical Possibility. *Man* (n.s.) 11:463–91.

Spencer, Jonathan.
    1989   Anthropology as a Kind of Writing. *Man* (n. s.) 24: 145–64

Spiro, Melford E.
    1986   Cultural Relativism and the Future of Anthropology, *Cultural Anthropology* 1:3:259–86.

Strathern, Marilyn.
    1987   Out of Context: The Persuasive Fiction of Anthropology. *Current Anthropology* 28:3:251–81.

Thornton, Robert.
    1983   Narrative Ethnography in Africa, 1850–1920: The Creation and Capture of an Appropriate Domain for Anthropology. *Man* (n.s.) 18:3:502–20.

Toulmin, Stephen Edelston.
    1958   *The Uses of Argument.* Cambridge: Cambridge University Press.
    1979   *An Introduction to Reasoning.* New York: Macmillan Publishing Co.

Turner, Victor W.
    1957   *Schism and Continuity in an African Society.* Manchester: Manchester University Press.

Van Maanen, John.
    1988   *Tales of the Field: On Writing Ethnography.* Chicago: The University of Chicago Press.

Van Velsen, Jaap.
    1967   The Extended-Case Method and Situational Analysis. In *The Craft of Social Anthropology,* edited by Arnold L. Epstein, 129–49. London: Tavistock Publications.

Vincent, Joan.
    1978   Political Anthropology: Manipulative Strategies. *Annual Review of Anthropology* 7:175–94.

Von Furer-Haimendorf, Christoph.
    1964   *The Sherpas of Nepal: Buddhist Highlanders.* Berkeley: University of California Press.

Walters, Ronald G.
    1980   Signs of the Times: Clifford Geertz and the Historians. *Social Research* 47:537–56.

Whitehead, Tony Larry, and Mary Ellen Conaway, eds.
    1986   *Self, Sex, and Gender in Cross-Cultural Fieldwork.* Urbana: University of Illinois Press.

Wilson, Monica.
    1951   *Good Company.* London: Oxford University Press.